book *of* faith
Lenten Journey

book *of* faith
Lenten Journey
Water Marks

Diane Jacobson

BOOK OF FAITH LENTEN JOURNEY
Water Marks

Text on pages 7–19 adapted from David L. Miller, *Book of Faith Lenten Journey: Marks of the Christian* (Augsburg Fortress, 2009); Henry F. French, *Book of Faith Lenten Journey: 40 Days with the Lord's Prayer* (Augsburg Fortress, 2009); and Ron Klug, *How to Keep a Spiritual Journal* (Augsburg Books, 1993).

For information on the Book of Faith initiative and Book of Faith resources, go to www.bookoffaith.org.

Book of Faith is an initiative of the

 Evangelical Lutheran Church in America
God's work. Our hands.

Cover design: Joe Vaughan
Interior design: Ivy Palmer Skrade
Typesetting: Timothy W. Larson

Library of Congress Cataloging-in-Publication Data
Jacobson, Diane L., 1948-
 Book of faith Lenten journey : water marks / Diane Jacobson.
    p. cm.
 Includes bibliographical references.
 ISBN 978-1-4514-0262-9 (alk. paper)
 1. Bible—Criticism, interpretation, etc.—Textbooks. 2. Bible—Devotional use. 3. Evangelical Lutheran Church in America—Doctrines. I. Title. II. Title: Lenten journey.
 BS511.3.J34 2011
 242'.34—dc23   2011029414

Manufactured in the U.S.A.

15   14   13   12   11   1   2   3   4   5   6   7   8   9   10

Contents

Our Writer

Diane Jacobson is director of the Book of Faith Initiative for the ELCA. She is professor emeritus of Old Testament at Luther Seminary in Saint Paul, Minnesota, where she taught 1982–2010. She co-authored *Opening the Book of Faith: Lutheran Insights for Bible Study* (2008) and served on the consulting board and as a contributor to *Lutheran Study Bible* (2009). She is, first and foremost, a lover of Scripture. "I'm in love with this Book," she says. "My calling is to teach Scripture for the sake of God's world, and to invite others into the wonders and rewards of exploring the Bible together."

The worship helps and suggestions that accompany the seven weekly themes of *Water Marks* were prepared by *Paul Jacobson*. He has served as a church musician in New York and taught music theory and composition at Concordia College, Bronxville, NY. Paul has been a soloist with baroque ensembles throughout the U.S.A. and abroad, and in 1985 he co-founded The Lyra Baroque Orchestra of Minnesota. In addition to his performing career Paul writes hymns and other liturgical music and leads worship and music for various church gatherings. He has a special interest in historical flutes.

The worship helps can be downloaded for free at www.augsburgfortress.org. Search for the title *Water Marks*. Click on the title and then open the "Worship Helps" tab in the product description.

Preface

For the last five years, I have been privileged to serve as the director of the Book of Faith Initiative of the Evangelical Lutheran Church in America (ELCA). This initiative was begun both to affirm the centrality of the Bible to Christian life and faith and also to address the lack of biblical knowledge and engagement in many parts of our church. The work has been both exciting and inspiring.

The purpose of the Book of Faith Initiative is to increase biblical literacy and fluency for the sake of the world (see www.bookoffaith.org). The Evangelical Lutheran Church in America has made a commitment to encourage all members of our congregations, from children to adults, to dig deeper into our book of faith, the Bible. The Book of Faith Initiative recommends a new model for our church: a grass-roots approach embracing a common vision in which all are invited to open Scripture and join the conversation. Each community is encouraged to decide how the Book of Faith Initiative will become a vital part of its own ministry.

Our conviction is that as the language of the Bible becomes more and more our native tongue, it will continually shape how we think and speak about God, about the world, and about ourselves. As we immerse ourselves in Scripture, Christ, the incarnate Word of God and center of our faith, is birthed within us. The Bible invites us into a relationship with God, making demands on our lives and promising us life in Christ. The Bible tells the stories of people living their faith over the centuries and, through its demands and promises, forms us as a people of faith. We become renewed, enlivened, and empowered as God, through Scripture, forms our hearts, our minds, our community conversation, and our commitments.

My hope is that this volume, *Book of Faith Lenten Journey: Water Marks*, might help you, in your own context, to live into the commitments of the initiative and accomplish our common purpose. This book will engage you in an encounter with the active power of the Word of God. Each week the journey uses scriptural passages to explore one of the many ways God's Word is at work in the world and in our lives.

You can use *Book of Faith Lenten Journey: Water Marks* on your own, with your family at home, together with a spiritual friend or small group, or with your entire congregation. Related worship helps and sermon starters for mid-week Lenten worship are available online (see location on "Our Writers" page). Be sure to visit the Book of Faith Web site regularly for more resources designed to bring the book of faith and the community of faith closer together.

Introduction

Water is nearly everywhere. Water surrounds us in our natural world, in oceans, rivers, and lakes. Water marks our natural lives from our mother's wombs to our daily bathing and the quenching of our thirst. Water marks our sacramental lives in God as we die and rise with Christ at our baptisms. And so it is with Scripture: from the first chapter of the Bible to the last, God's Word is water marked.

In this book of Lenten devotions you are invited into this reality. You are invited to hear and experience God's Word for us through a myriad of passages about water. In fact, these water passages will invite you on a biblical journey from Old Testament stories of creation and redemption to the words of the prophets and the prayers of the Psalms; from stories of water in the lives of Christ's disciples to the centrality of water in the life of Christ himself. Through this one image of water you will immerse yourselves in a forty-day overview of all of Scripture.

On this journey with and through the Bible, you are invited to bring your own experiences of water. Remember your first swimming lesson or fishing trip, your first or most exciting ride on a boat. Remember the times water has been threatening or life-giving. Remember floods and the fear of drowning. Remember that time you were dying of thirst and someone offered you a cool glass of water. On this journey, bring along your tears of joy and sorrow. And in, with, and under it all, remember your baptism and the daily calling to live out your baptism in your daily life. Let the waters of your life and the waters of your baptism intermingle with the waters of Scripture.

Throughout this journey with Scripture, do not worry about what you do not already know. Do not be afraid of making mistakes or asking questions. It might be helpful to remember that Martin Luther translated the Old and New

Testaments from Hebrew and Greek into the common language, German, so that more people could read the Scriptures for themselves. Luther wanted to make sure not only that people could read the Scriptures, but also that they benefited from what they read. In 1521 he wrote "A Brief Instruction on What to Look for and Expect in the Gospels." This little booklet was intended to help preachers, hearers, and readers of the Word focus on how the Scriptures—both Old and New Testaments—bring us the good news of Jesus Christ, who is God's living gift of grace to the church, to the world, and to each one of us personally. The book of devotions you are holding shares that same purpose: to help you read and reflect on the Scriptures, expecting to receive from them the gift of God's grace through faith in Jesus Christ.

Praying the Scriptures with Luther and His Barber

In addition to advice on how to read the Scriptures, Luther also offered advice on how to pray. Luther's barber, Peter, had asked him how an ordinary person—not a pastor or a scholar of religion—should pray. In response, Luther wrote *A Simple Way to Pray*, in which he encouraged Christians to pray in their own words, rather than reciting prayers they had memorized, and to trust the Holy Spirit to guide them.

Christians today typically have more experience with personal prayer than did the ordinary men and women of Luther's day, who would have known only the Our Father, the Hail Mary, and a few other prayers heard at mass or taught for private devotion. Even for us, though, it is easy to feel uncomfortable and inadequate in our praying. Luther offered Peter—and us—a simple, concrete way to enter more deeply and personally into prayer. He suggested starting with a text—from the Scriptures, the catechism, or other devotional material such as hymns—and reading it in four ways:

- Read it as a schoolbook, reflecting upon what God is teaching you.
- Read it as a song or praise book, giving thanks to God for the gifts God gives or brings to your awareness.

- Read it as a penitential book, confessing to God your sins, your needs, and your weaknesses as they are revealed in your reflection.
- Turn the words into a short prayer you may speak to God.

There are no right and wrong prayers in this approach. "Rather do I want your heart to be stirred and guided,"[1] Luther wrote to his friend.

Luther's core conviction is that the Scriptures are not intended to fill our heads with interesting ideas, but to bring the active power of God's Word into our lives. Bible study and prayer belong together. Worship is also a part of this dynamic encounter. Christians through the ages have recognized that what we believe shapes how we worship and also that how we worship shapes what we believe. Over time, what we say, do, sing, hear, and experience in worship influences us and forms our faith. For this reason Luther did not stop with translating the Scriptures into German. He also translated the worship service into the language of the people. He incorporated congregational singing into the liturgy and composed new hymns to teach the Christian faith through song. Because one of the ways we hear and experience the wonders of the Word is through song, you will find hymns woven through this Lenten journey.

We are a church committed to opening Scripture together and joining in conversation about its meaning for our lives. As you embark on this forty-day period of devotion, I invite you to come to your encounter with Scripture with a particular set of attitudes:

- Come *prayerfully*, asking that the Holy Spirit might guide you and that Christ might be with you.
- Come *humbly*, asking for the gift of faith and ever mindful of your own capacity for sin and self-deceit. Luther said: "The Holy Scriptures require a humble reader who shows reverence and fear toward the Word of God, and constantly says, 'Teach me, teach me, teach me.' . . . The Spirit resists the proud."[2]
- Come *mindfully*, bringing to your study the gifts of reason, the tools of scholarship, and the insights of others.
- Come *attentively*, reading Scripture carefully and closely.

- Come *collectively* in the context of a faithful community, letting your own stories interact with the stories of the Bible.
- Come *expectantly*, listening for the voice of God working through the text to inspire, shape, and enliven you individually and in your community of faith.

"Let the word of Christ dwell in you richly; teach and admonish one another in all wisdom; and with gratitude in your hearts sing psalms, hymns, and spiritual songs to God" (Colossians 3:16).

How to Use This Book

Your forty-day Lenten journey will mark you with water from the pages of Scripture and invite you daily to remember your baptism. This journey will encourage you to listen to God's Spirit speaking in your own heart and experience. It will help you pay attention to what God is saying to you, is asking of you, is confirming in you, and is working in you. This journey will support your honest wrestling with God and help you to exercise your faith through conversation and prayer. In this way, your relationship with God will be watered through the roots of Scripture so that it may blossom and grow fruit, leading you to love the world as God loves it.

You will probably benefit most by fixing a special time of day to spend time with this book and your Bible. It is easier—especially in the beginning—to maintain a spiritual practice if you do it regularly at the same time. For many people, morning, while the house is still quiet and before the busyness of the day begins, is a good time. Others will find that the noon hour or before bedtime serves well. If you are working through this book with a partner, a group, or as family devotions, you might gather in the morning or before or after a meal. Do whatever works for you to maintain a regular, daily encounter with God. You might also set apart a special place with a candle and a basin of water. You can begin each water-marked day by dipping your finger into the water and making a sign of the cross on your forehead or on the forehead of your conversation partner.

You will note that there are no readings for Sunday. The forty days of Lent traditionally exclude Sundays, the day we celebrate the resurrection of Christ.

Although this book is designed to be used during the forty days of Lent, it can be used at any time of the year. If you pick a time other than Lent for your journey, it would still be best to walk day-by-day through the book. Each day's devotion offers plenty of rich resources for you to ponder. There is no need to rush. For this reason, if you are not able to read through *Water Marks* in forty days, feel free to slow down and take a longer period of time. It is better to complete the journey at your own pace than to give it up partway through. Set a schedule that works for you, and be as consistent as you can.

The amount of time you spend in devotions each day is entirely up to you. Sometimes you may only have a few minutes. And sometimes you might find it fruitful to spend more than one day with a particular reflection, question, or quotation that stirs you. If one element speaks more deeply to you than others—blessing, challenging, or troubling you—spend time with it. Always go where there is fruit. Don't worry that the other elements don't touch your mind and heart that day. Go where Christ is pleased to speak and give himself to you. Luther wrote, "If you pause here and let him do you good, that is if you believe that he benefits and helps you, then you really have it. The Christ is yours, presented to you as a gift."[1]

The Daily Plan

Each day of the journey begins with a short scriptural passage, followed by a brief reflection on that passage. These daily passages and reflections are intended to stir your own thinking and meditation, so read slowly. You may want to read through each passage and reflection more than once, perhaps even reading them aloud so that you might hear the text as well as seeing it on the page. Let the words sink into your consciousness. Take time to consider and benefit from what God is saying to you and in you.

Following the daily reflection, you will find *Biblical Wisdom* and a brief passage from another place in the Scriptures that relates to the meditation. It may be obvious to you how this second passage relates to the day's theme, or you may need to think about it for a while before you make a connection. Either way, read the biblical text slowly. Let it speak to you.

After the second scriptural passage, you will find *Wisdom from the Tradition*. This wisdom may be brief quotations from scholars and theologians from throughout Christian history or hymns verses, both ancient and contemporary.

These quotations stand in conversation with the biblical verses and the reflections, so take time to dwell in these as well.

Next comes *Silence for Meditation.* Some of you may already be steeped in a tradition of meditation involving getting centered, breathing slowly and deeply, focusing your attention, and taking time to be silent and listen. Others may be uncomfortable with such practices. One of the rich insights coming from a number of spiritual practice traditions is the importance of learning how to be still, how to listen within the silence, and how to quiet the mind and body. Just as public worship needs silence amidst the prayer and song, so also does private devotion. Silence leaves room for the Spirit to live and breathe and have its being. Think of silence as a time of refreshment, a time of re-spiriting, if you will.

Once you feel yourself settling down, slowly look a second time over the daily meditation, the scriptural passages, and the theological thought. Note the words, thoughts, images, and feelings that draw you. Explore meanings and implications for your life. Jot down any insights that occur to you. Do the readings raise questions for you? Do they suggest some action or response? Write them down or discuss them with your devotion partners. Stay with the meditation time as long as it feels useful. When you are ready to move on, you might close your eyes, observe your breath for a minute, and thank God for the gift of life and the gift of God's Word.

Then move on to the *Psalm Fragment.* The psalms are both our words to God and God's words to us. They have been a mainstay of prayer for Jewish and Christian believers, speaking the deepest hope, joy, and pain of our lives. Read the *Psalm Fragment* silently or aloud, and reflect for a moment on how the psalm connects to the passage of the day and moves us toward prayer.

In the section *Questions to Ponder* you will find several questions related to the day's readings. The questions use the insights of the readings to draw you into your own experience, so you may see where and how God is working in your life and in our world. These questions may be used for personal reflection, as a basis for conversation with others, or as prompts to respond to in your journal. You need not answer every question. Choose those that draw you in and deepen your conversation with God and other people. The questions provided in this book may also lead you to ask your own questions. Again, go where there is fruit.

The final heading is *Prayer for Today*, a one- or two-line prayer to end your session. If you prefer, you can articulate and pray your own short prayer based on your own reflections. You might choose to repeat this prayer from time to time throughout the day.

Hints on Keeping a Journal

Journaling as a spiritual practice can be profoundly transforming. It can keep us more closely in touch with ourselves and our response to God over time. Sometimes we don't really know or understand our thoughts and feelings until we write them down and look at what flows from the pen or through our fingers on the keyboard. We may be surprised to see what is actually moving and happening in us. Then we can draw insight and consolation from what God is saying and doing.

Keeping a journal can also be a form of prayer, a powerful way of getting to know yourself—and God—more deeply. Journaling helps you focus and clarify your thoughts, while keeping a record of your insights, questions, and prayers. It may lead you to thoughts and awareness that will surprise you. As you write, you can respond to God with your thanks and pleas, your joys and sorrows, offering them all to God.

A Few Hints for Journaling

1. Write freely. Ignore your inner critic. Don't worry about grammar, literary style, whether you are writing in complete sentences, or what it sounds like. Just write! Simply get in touch with an idea, emotion, image, or memory and begin writing. Describe what you notice, how you feel, and how something is affecting you. From time to time, read back over your words to see what is happening more clearly.
2. Be honest with God. Do not censor yourself! Don't write what you think you're supposed to believe or feel or think. Don't write what you think is

acceptable to your spouse or friends, your pastor, or your fourth-grade teacher. Write your real thoughts, feelings, beliefs, and experiences as far as you can identify them. When you are uncertain, write your confusion and questions. Your relationship with God will be as real and honest as you are.

3. Begin and end your journaling with prayer. Ask for insight to see God's work more clearly, to notice what is really going on beneath the surface of your days and thoughts. At the end, thank God for what guidance, wisdom, or consolation has come through your writing.

4. Feel free to address God directly in your writing. You may choose to write your entire journal entry as a prayer. Share what is happening to you and in you, what you are noticing in your journey with this book. Like the psalmists and Job, hold nothing back. You may be surprised by what bubbles out of you.

5. Don't worry or stop if your journaling takes you in directions beyond the suggestions in this book. Go where you are led. Notice what you notice. The Holy Spirit will lead you to places where you may drink from the living waters Christ Jesus offers. This book's journaling ideas and *Questions to Ponder* are suggestions for your writing. Don't hesitate to move in other directions when promising avenues appear.

6. You may wish to carry this book and your notebook or journal with you every day during your journey (but keep them safe from prying eyes). Your Lenten journey can be an intense experience that doesn't stop when you close the book. When your mind and heart are stirred during the day, it is helpful to be able to write notes or new journal entries as they occur to you.

Journeying with Others

You can use this book (and I hope you do) with another person or with your family or a small group. If you wish, each person can first do his or her own reading, reflection, and writing in solitude. When you come together, you can share the insights you have gained from your time alone. Your discussion can focus on any of the elements of each day's journey.

Questions to Ponder is a natural place to start discussions with a group or spiritual friend. However, you might find that a section from a daily reflection, *Biblical Wisdom*, or *Wisdom from the Tradition* has particularly stirred one of you. If so, start there, and let the discussion flow in the directions that are most fruitful for the needs and questions of the group. Trust that God's Word will bear good fruit in your conversation.

If you are working through the book with people you trust, you may feel comfortable sharing some of what you have written in your journal. But no one should ever be pressured to do this. It should also be a ground rule that whatever is said in a small group stays within the group.

Always remember that your goal is to grow in relation with Christ and his church and in your understanding of God's Word. You gather to learn from one another, not to argue or to prove that you are right and the other is wrong. Practice listening and trying to understand why your discussion partner or small-group members think as they do.

Sharing your experiences is a way of encouraging and guiding one another. It provides the opportunity to offer feedback gently and to help one another translate insight into action.

By all means, pray with others. This strengthens the spiritual bonds among those who take the journey together. Spend a few moments sharing prayer requests around the theme of the day. Then pray for one another and your faith community as you bring your time together to a close.

Week One
Water Marks God's Creation

Day 1

God Stirs the Waters

Day 2

Water Marks God's Great Battle

Day 3

Water Marks the Flood

Day 4

Water Marks the Stream in the Midst of the Garden

Day 5

Water Marks the Great Rivers

Day 6

The River Brings Hope to the City of God

Day 1—Ash Wednesday
God Stirs the Waters

In the beginning when God created the heavens and the earth, the earth
was a formless void and darkness covered the face of the deep, while a
wind from God swept over the face of the waters.
   Genesis 1:1-2

Our journey begins at the beginning with God hovering, like a mother bird, over the unformed waters, ready to begin the great journey of creation. The waters are already there. The waters are both the deep chaos always ready for battle and the unformed nothingness that waits for God's Word to become part of creation.

In preparation for speaking the world into existence, God is already there as wind, as breath, as Spirit—all three realities present in the underlying Hebrew word *ru'ah [ROO-ah]*. This *ru'ah* of God is God's breath pushing back the chaotic waters, to keep them from breaking free. This *ru'ah* of God is the wind of God stirring up the stagnant waters of nothingness so that they might receive the breath of life.

This *ru'ah* of God is the Holy Spirit, brooding over the waters, preparing for the birth of all living things. At the beginning of our journey marked by water, these three pictures of God at work in creation call to mind God's activity with us through our own baptismal waters. As in creation, God's breath surrounds our own chaos—our sin—and puts it to death. We die with Christ. And for our own sake and the sake of the ongoing life of our community and world, we are, like the chaotic waters of creation, constrained and given limits.

As in creation, God's wind stirs us up and awakens us. Where there was nothingness, now we are poised, ready to be born, ready to become the something God would have us be. And by that same Spirit we are made alive. We are like newborn infants spanked as we first face the world, so that we take our first gorgeous gulps of fresh air. In the waters of baptism we are blessed as new creations and called to joy and relationship and fruitful activity.

Biblical Wisdom

"Or who shut in the sea with doors when it burst out from the womb?—when I made the clouds its garment, and thick darkness its swaddling band, and prescribed bounds for it, and set bars and doors, and said, 'Thus far shall you come, and no farther, and here shall your proud waves be stopped'? "
Job 38:8-11

Wisdom from the Tradition

As a hen broods her eggs, keeping them warm in order to hatch her chicks, and, as it were, to bring them to life through heat, so Scripture says the Holy Spirit brooded, as it were, on the waters to bring to life those substances which were to be quickened and adorned. For it is the office of the Holy Spirit to make alive.[1]
Martin Luther

Silence for Meditation

Psalm Fragment

By the word of the LORD the heavens were made,
and all their host by the breath of his mouth.
He gathered the waters of the sea as in a bottle;
he put the deeps in storehouses.
Psalm 33:6-7

Questions to Ponder

- How do you imagine God's Spirit working to create something new out of unformed waters of creation?
- How does this relate to the Holy Spirit working in you through your baptism and in your community?
- What formless or void spaces need to be shaped or reshaped in you?

Prayer for Today

Creator God—Father, Son, and Holy Spirit—restrain me, birth me, and stir me to life this day and always. Amen.

Day 2—Thursday
Water Marks God's Great Battle

By his power he stilled the Sea;
by his understanding he struck down Rahab.
By his wind the heavens were made fair;
his hand pierced the fleeing serpent.
    Job 26:12-13

Children are not the only ones who understand the reality of monsters. Behind the imagery of waters of the deep in Genesis 1:2 lies a long tradition throughout the ancient Near East that the sea is a monster that must be contained or even killed by God in order to insure that God's created world is a good and ordered place. In the Old Testament this monster is named Leviathan or Rahab or Lotan or simply the Deep. We also know this monster as Satan or the devil.

We recognize this monster. We experience this monster in floods and terrorism, in starvation and adultery, in hatred and abuse. We see the monster in the world and name it as evil. And what is more, we see it in ourselves and name it as sin. Two things about this monster remain terribly scary. First, we look around us at the world and the monster so often appears to be stronger than God. Second, we look deep within ourselves and wonder if even God can defeat such an insidious beast.

But wonder of wonders, God speaks to our fears. God has contained the mighty waters since the beginning of time. Again and again, God meets the devil and will not be deceived. And God in Christ, through the cross, has taken up our monstrous sins and tamed them through forgiveness. When we experience such wonders, we join Job and the psalmists, and the writer of Revelation in giving thanks to God for the monster's defeat.

Biblical Wisdom

The great dragon was thrown down, that ancient serpent, who is called
the Devil and Satan, the deceiver of the whole world—he was thrown
down to the earth, and his angels were thrown down with him.
    Revelation 12:9

Wisdom from the Tradition

For thou goest down into the water, bearing thy sins, but the invocation of grace, having sealed thy soul, suffereth thee not afterwards to be swallowed up by the terrible dragon. Having gone down dead in sins, thou comest up quickened in righteousness. For if thou hast been united with the likeness of the Saviour's death, thou shalt also be deemed worthy of His Resurrection.[2]

St. Cyril of Jerusalem

Silence for Meditation

Psalm Fragment

You divided the sea by your might;

you broke the heads of the dragons in the waters.

Psalm 74:13

Questions to Ponder

- What "monsters" are alive and well in the world?
- What monsters do you experience in yourself? Are you comforted by God's promise that these monsters have been and will continue to be defeated?

Prayer for Today

We give you thanks, O God of might, that you have met the monsters around us and within us and have defeated Leviathan once and for all time. Amen.

Day 3—Friday
Water Marks the Flood

The flood continued forty days on the earth; and the waters increased. . . . And all flesh died that moved on the earth. . . . But God remembered Noah. . . and the waters gradually receded from the earth. . . . When I bring clouds over the earth and the bow is seen in the clouds, I will remember my covenant that is between me and you and every living creature of all flesh; and the waters shall never again become a flood to destroy all flesh.

Genesis 7:17, 21; 8:1, 3; 9:14-15

Nearly every child knows the story of Noah's ark. Many versions of the ancient boat with its friendly animals and congenial Noah and family have been made into a delightful toy for kids. But in truth this story is quite frightening. In the biblical account, the waters of chaos become the instrument of God's destruction, and all flesh is destroyed.

We glimpse water's destructive power in deadly tsunamis or in rivers swelling over their banks and flooding our towns. These watery terrors may cause some to wonder if such flooding is indeed the judgment of God responding in righteous anger at our unabated pride, our continued injustice, and our apparent lack of concern for the earth and for one another.

And yet the account of the flood is also a tale of promise. God looks on the water's destruction and vows, "Never again!" God first remembers Noah and is filled with compassion. Then God sees the rainbow, the sign of the covenant, and remembers the divine promise. Abundant, fruitful, and ongoing life is the will of God. The dove of peace with the olive branch in her beak joins the rainbow as God's sign that the chaotic waters will never again have the final say.

Perhaps we do not have it wrong after all when we give Noah's ark to our children. They, like us, will come to know the horrors of floods. But through their play they know something more real. They know that the picture of harmonious creation with animals walking two by two is a water mark of promise.

Biblical Wisdom

> You cast me into the deep, into the heart of the seas, and the flood
>   surrounded me;
>   all your waves and your billows passed over me. . . .
> Then the LORD spoke to the fish, and it spewed Jonah out upon the
>   dry land
>   Jonah 2:3, 10

Wisdom from the Tradition

What meets us here is proclamation, the announcement of what God has done about a fractured world. . . . The flood has effected no change in humankind. But it has effected an irreversible change in God. . . . It is God's remembering, and only that, which gives hope and makes new life possible.[3]

Walter Brueggemann

Silence for Meditation

Psalm Fragment

> *The LORD sits enthroned over the flood;*
>> *the LORD sits enthroned as king forever.*
>
> Psalm 29:10

Questions to Ponder

- How does the biblical story of Noah's flood offer both warning and promise?
- What do you see when a rainbow appears after a storm?
- How do we teach and learn from our children as we play with a toy ark?

Prayer for Today

God of judgment and mercy, protect us from the floods all around us. Look to your rainbow and remember your promise this day and always. This we ask in Christ's name. Amen.

Day 4—Saturday
Water Marks the Stream in the Midst of the Garden

> *No plant of the field was yet in the earth and no herb of the field had yet sprung up—for the LORD God had not caused it to rain upon the earth, and there was no one to till the ground; but a stream would rise from the earth, and water the whole face of the ground.*
>
> Genesis 2:5-6

We've looked at water's destructive power. But we know that water gives life. In fact, without water living things cannot live. Modern science tells us that all living things are made up mostly of water, anywhere from around 60 percent of an adult human being to 95 percent of some plants. So it is small wonder that before any tree or plant or creature is found in the primeval garden, there is a stream that rises up and waters all the earth. The beautiful painting called *The Garden of Earthly Delights*, by Hieronymous Bosch, pictures this breathtaking scene. With this single image, the very substance that most threatens the created order in Genesis 1 is transformed into the source of life in Genesis 2.

If we have eyes to see, this dual reality of water is all around us. Our oceans teem with life as well as threaten. Our rivers both overflow and offer cultivation and transport. We are all brought to life in the midst of our mothers' chaotic waters. Proverbs 18:4 uses this contrasting image of water to teach us that our words can both drown the other as well as gush with wisdom.

Isn't it astounding that God has made creation in such a way? The same substance gives both death and life. Paradox stands at the heart of creation, just as it stands at the heart of God's central act of salvation. The cross of Christ, the very instrument of death, is, at the same time, the tree that gives us life. This dual reality of cross and water, this paradox of death and life, marks our baptism and the journey that follows. We die with Christ, and in Christ we are reborn.

Biblical Wisdom

> The words of the mouth are deep waters;
> the fountain of wisdom is a gushing stream.
> Proverbs 18:4

Wisdom from the Tradition

Hope blooms in a weary world when creatures, once forlorn, find wilderness reborn.
Hope blooms in a weary world: the promised green of Eden comes.
The trees shall clap their hands; the dry lands, gush with springs;
The hills and mountains shall break forth with singing!
We shall go out in joy, and be led forth in peace, as all the world in wonder echoes shalom.[4]

Mary Louise Bringle

Silence for Meditation

Psalm Fragment

> *He turns a desert into pools of water,*
> *a parched land into springs of water.*
> Psalm 107:35

Questions to Ponder
- What images come to mind when you hear the phrase "life-giving water"?
- What, if any, paradoxes (contradictions) stand at the heart of your life and faith? How do you live with these?

Prayer for Today
God of grace, grant us this day the gift of seeing your life-giving waters all around us. Refresh us through your fountains and streams that we might recognize your abundance.

Day 5—Monday
Water Marks the Great Rivers

> *A river flows out of Eden to water the garden, and from there it divides*
> *and becomes four branches. The name of the first is Pishon. . . . The*
> *name of the second river is Gihon. . . . The name of the third river is Tigris.*
> *. . . And the fourth river is the Euphrates.*
> Genesis 2:10-11, 13-14

Quite often we skip the part of Genesis 2 that lists the four rivers in Eden. We never find these verses in our lectionary texts, probably because they may seem less significant than the creation of Adam and Eve and the presence of the trees of knowledge and of life. But let's pause for a moment to consider where these verses take us.

A river flows out of Eden. Geographically, the river first waters the garden and then divides into four great rivers. While we know the location of the Tigris and Euphrates Rivers still today (in modern Iraq), the identities of the Gihon (in

Jerusalem or Ethiopia) and the Pishon have given rise to much speculation. What is clear is that these rivers are real rivers found in the world. Some have speculated on their reality to try to discover where the Garden of Eden may have been. But a better path is to take heart in observation that the waters from Eden do not stay there. These real rivers water the whole world, making possible life beyond the garden. That four crucial rivers come from the very first river God creates points us to the reality that the whole earth is the Lord's.

A river flows out of Eden. Scripturally, it feeds our hope for the promised future. The prophet Ezekiel envisions such a life-giving stream flowing from the temple (Ezekiel 47:1-12). This river will make the salt water fresh, will be the home for swarms of fish, and will supply water to the roots of the trees along the bank. This river that flows out of Eden also flows from the throne of God. The picture of Eden is not only about a distant, mythic past; it is also about a divinely promised future.

So it is that this river of Eden feeds both our current reality, where we live, and our hope for what God has in store for all the world.

Biblical Wisdom

Wherever the river goes, every living creature that swarms will live, and there will be very many fish, once these waters reach there. It will become fresh; and everything will live where the river goes.
Ezekiel 47:9

Wisdom from the Tradition

What an inexpressible amount of water was in Paradise, if the river, after having watered the garden, could still enclose the entire world with four arms and fructify it! All the water outside of Paradise, which supplies all civilizations, is, so to speak, only a remainder or residue from the water of Paradise![5]
Gerhard von Rad

Silence for Meditation

Psalm Fragment

The earth is the LORD's and all that is in it,

the world, and those who live in it;

for he has founded it on the seas,

and established it on the rivers.

Psalm 24:1-2

Questions to Ponder

- Which four great rivers of the world could you name, and what goes on near those rivers?
- In what ways does the story of Eden's great river strike you as a story about the past, present, and future?
- How do God's life-giving waters flow to you, and through you?

Prayer for Today

Source of life, we thank you for the gift of the great rivers of our world. May they inspire in us joy in your creation and hope for the future you have promised. Amen.

Day 6—Tuesday
The River Brings Hope to the City of God

God is our refuge and strength, a very present help in trouble.

Therefore we will not fear, though the earth should change,

though the mountains shake in the heart of the sea;

though its waters roar and foam, though the mountains tremble with

its tumult.

There is a river whose streams make glad the city of God,

the holy habitation of the Most High.

God is in the midst of the city; it shall not be moved. . . .

Psalm 46:1-5

So many of our cities and towns are found by rivers. Think of the great cities scattered along the Mississippi or Columbia Rivers, the Rio Grande, Ohio, or Susquehanna. We know why this is true. Without water, the source of life, a city cannot thrive.

The principal biblical city is Jerusalem, city of God. Jerusalem, like other cities, was founded by a river, really more a stream, called the Gihon. This river is said to flow beneath the temple, and in Ezekiel's vision, which we looked at yesterday, it becomes the river of hope from Eden. This river is also said to point to the Messiah, to be the place that will mark the true king. And, indeed, the Gihon feeds the Pool of Siloam where Jesus joins his own saliva with the waters from the stream and heals the man born blind (John 9:11).

In Psalm 46 this river of Jerusalem becomes for us a sign that the watery chaos that has threatened from the beginning of time is no match for God. The streams of the river make the city glad. God, the ultimate source of life, is in the midst of the city. Though life's waters roar and foam, God is our refuge and strength. This psalm has been a comfort to many throughout the ages, including Martin Luther, who used it as the basis of his hymn "A Mighty Fortress Is Our God." And the river of hope becomes, in the hymn of John Newton, the grace that springs from eternal love. How astounding it is that God gives us this concrete sign of hope so we might know that God is in our midst even when steeples are falling.

Biblical Wisdom

When he had said this, he spat on the ground and made mud with the saliva and spread the mud on the man's eyes, saying to him, "Go, wash in the pool of Siloam" (which means Sent). Then he went and washed and came back able to see.
John 9:6-7

Wisdom from the Tradition

See, the streams of living waters, springing from eternal love,
well supply your sons and daughters, and all fear of want remove.
Who can faint, while such a river ever will our thirst assuage?
Grace which, like the Lord, the giver, never fails from age to age.[6]
John Newton

Silence for Meditation

Psalm Fragment

He will drink from the stream by the path;
therefore he will lift up his head.
Psalm 110:7

Questions to Ponder

- How can we see physical rivers and other realities of nature as signs of God's presence with us?
- Have you experienced gladness "streaming" from God? If so, when and how?
- What sort of water is marking your life at this time—stormy waves, clear cool streams, quiet lakes? What kind of waters do you long for?

Prayer for Today

God of grace, be with us where we live. Gladden our hearts and help us to see the signs of your presence all around us. This we ask in Christ's name. Amen.

Week Two
Water Marks Israel's Story and Our Story

Day 7
Water Marks the Birth of the Deliverer

Day 8
Water Marks the Meeting at the Well

Day 9
The Water Is Stained with Blood

Day 10
Water Marks Victory at Sea

Day 11
Water Comes from the Rock

Day 12
Water Marks Crossing to the Promised Land

Day 7—Wednesday
Water Marks the Birth of the Deliverer

Pharaoh commanded all his people, "Every boy that is born to the
Hebrews you shall throw into the Nile. . . . The woman conceived and bore
a son. . . . When she could hide him no longer she got a papyrus basket
for him . . . she put the child in it and placed it among the reeds on the
bank of the river. . . . The daughter of Pharaoh came down to bathe at the
river. . . . She saw the basket . . . opened it, [and] she saw the child. He was
crying, and she took pity on him, "This must be one of the Hebrews' chil-
dren," she said, . . . and she took him as her son. She named him Moses
"because," she said, "I drew him out of the water."
Exodus 1:22; 2:2-3, 5-6, 10

In the story of God's people water becomes a threat in the land of Egypt. Pharaoh, the embodiment of earthly tyranny, threatens to drown all newborn Hebrew boys. But God has a surprise. God blesses a Hebrew woman with a child, and she builds a basket (ark) to hide him. In Hebrew the word for this basket is the same as the one used for the saving ark of Noah. The Hebrew mother gently places the child in the midst of the very same river intended by evil for drowning.

Ironically, it is the tyrant Pharaoh's own daughter who comes down to the river to bathe. She sees the child and is bathed by compassion and insight. This daughter of Pharaoh, this foreigner, becomes a daughter of God, herself adopted into the people of God. In turn, she adopts and names the child "Moses" (*mosheh*), which in Egyptian means "son" and also sounds like the Hebrew word for "I drew out" (*mashah*). Think of it. Moses is himself drawn out of the water and is stamped with a name forever. This same Moses will grow up to be the one to lead his own people through the waters of death into freedom and new life.

What a water story! It's like the story of baptism, where we experience water marks of danger and birth, fear and compassion, death and triumphant new life. It is in these waters that we are adopted into God's family and named into a calling of service for the sake of the world. Like Moses, our birth itself is a gift. We are born into a world of potential danger and untold obstacles, but we are surrounded with unexpected women and men who meet us with compassion. We are also met by the one who draws us out of death into new life. Thanks be to God!

Biblical Wisdom

When Israel was a child, I loved him, and out of Egypt I called my son.
Hosea 11:1

Wisdom from the Tradition

Once again Pharaoh's plan has been thwarted and in a doubly miraculous way. The child has been rescued from exposure, even by the very daughter of the one who made the decree. God's plan for his people rested on the helpless child, floating down the river. But the child is not lost, and the story points expectantly toward the future.[7]

Brevard Childs

Silence for Meditation

Psalm Fragment

Your way was through the sea,
   your path, through the mighty waters;
   yet your footprints were unseen.
Psalm 77:19

Questions to Ponder
- What detail from the story of the birth of Moses most strikes you?
- What do you find most comforting or challenging about this story?
- How does this story touch your own story of birth, baptism, and calling?

Prayer for Today

Lord, we give you thanks for mothers and all women who are moved by compassion and insight. May we also dare to draw others out of danger and despair. Amen.

Day 8—Thursday
Water Marks the Meeting at the Well

> *[Moses] settled in the land of Midian, and sat down by a well. The priest of Midian had seven daughters. They came to draw water. . . . But some shepherds came and drove them away. Moses got up and came to their defense and watered their flock. When they returned to their father Reuel, . . . they said, "An Egyptian helped us against the shepherds; he even drew water for us and watered the flock." . . . He said, . . . "Invite him to break bread." . . . And he gave Moses his daughter Zipporah in marriage. She bore a son, and he named him Gershom; for he said, "I have been an alien residing in a foreign land."*
> Exodus 2:15-22

Have you ever noticed that almost every time the Bible tells us that a man sits down by a well, he ends up meeting a woman—and often getting married? Except Jesus, of course, though Jesus does talk about marriage to the Samaritan woman when they meet at the well. Each of these encounters teaches us something different. In this case, Moses is surrounded by seven women, the daughters of Reuel, just as he had been surrounded by women since his birth. And this story—like the story of his birth—again foreshadows Moses's calling of liberation through the water.

Two other interwoven themes also mark this meeting at the well. The first is the theme of hospitality. Moses the stranger, misidentified as an Egyptian, is invited to break bread with this Midianite family. Reuel offers Moses not only a meal, but also—as we have come to expect—the hand of his daughter in marriage.

The second theme is identification with the stranger. As important as the marriage is, the real climax of this encounter comes with the birth and naming of the child. Just as Moses's name had significance, so also does the name of his son, Gershom. The Hebrew word *ger* means "stranger," or "alien resident."

The name points to multiple meanings. Egypt's Pharaoh feared the growing Hebrew population in his country so much that he ordered the death of Hebrew babies, but Reuel, the priest of Midian, sees the stranger Moses not as one to fear but rather as one in need of hospitality. Through the naming of his son, Moses—as well as all of his Hebrew people—now are as marked forever with this alien-resident identity.

This story offers us an invitation that comes with our baptismal identity. Like Moses and the people of Israel, we are invited to identify with the alien resident, the stranger in our midst. And we are called to invite the stranger, the other, to feast at our table and to join with us as a company of strangers.

Biblical Wisdom

You shall also love the stranger, for you were strangers in the land of Egypt.
Deuteronomy 10:19

Wisdom from the Tradition

Let us remember the poor, and not forget kindness to strangers; above all, let us love God with all our soul, and might, and strength, and our neighbor as ourselves. So may we receive those things which the eye hath not seen, nor the ear heard, and which have not entered into the heart of man, which God hath prepared for those that love Him. . . . [8]

Athanasius

Silence for Meditation

Psalm Fragment

Wondrously show your steadfast love,
O savior of those who seek refuge
from their adversaries at your right hand.
Psalm 17:7

Questions to Ponder

- What meeting places in our culture might reflect the encounters in this story?
- What acts of hospitality to strangers do you remember?

- What does it mean to welcome alien residents or strangers into our midst? How well does your community or congregation do this?

Prayer for Today

Lord, teach us to identify with the stranger, and help us both to give and receive hospitality. This we ask in Christ's name. Amen.

Day 9—Friday
The Water Is Stained with Blood

> *Thus says the LORD, "By this you shall know that I am the LORD." See, with the staff that is in my hand I will strike the water that is in the Nile, and it shall be turned to blood. The fish in the river shall die, the river itself shall stink, and the Egyptians shall be unable to drink water from the Nile.*
> Exodus 7:17-18

Sometimes reading and understanding the Bible is not easy. Talking about the plagues that God unleashed on Egypt presents us with one of those difficult moments. The God we have come to know and love is "merciful and gracious, slow to anger, and abounding in steadfast love and faithfulness" (Exodus 34:6). So how can such a God have sent the plagues on Egypt? Perhaps it helps to see the plagues as a continuation of the cosmic battle against chaos. Pharaoh, the enslaver of the Israelites, is the human embodiment of chaos. The violence of the plagues serves justice. What's more, the Pharaoh of ancient Egypt saw himself as God, so this battle is fought to set the record straight. It is fought in order that all the world might know that the LORD, and not Pharaoh, is the one true God.

This first plague carries with it an enormous amount of symbolic weight that is centered around the understanding that blood, like water, holds both death and life. Look at the many connections. First, Pharaoh intended the Nile to be filled with the blood of the Israelites. Be careful what you wish for, answers God. Second, in the final plague—the death of the firstborn of the Egyptians (Exodus 12:29-32)—the Israelites mark their doorposts with blood to ward off the angel of death. Third, in the great victorious crossing of the sea, the blood of the Egyptians fills the waters when God closes the sea after the

Israelite people had safely passed. Finally, all of these together point us to God's final victory over evil when the blood of God's own beloved Son is spilled so that all might be saved.

None of this is easy. We wonder why new life must come from death. We wonder why blood must be spilled at all. If we were God, we would likely not have it be so, but so it is. There is blood in the water. But in both the blood of Christ Jesus and the waters of baptism, there is the promise of new life.

Biblical Wisdom

In him we have redemption through his blood, the forgiveness of our trespasses, according to the riches of his grace that he lavished on us.
Ephesians 1:7-8

Wisdom from the Tradition

The ultimate purpose of the sign is so that "you shall know that I am the LORD." . . . God asks that Israel be liberated from oppression to serve him. Pharaoh needs to recognize that this is an issue with cosmic implications. As Ezekiel 29:3 puts it, Pharaoh said, "The Nile is my own; I made it." God's action should show Pharaoh that the land of Egypt, its water, and its people are neither his creation nor his to do with as he pleases.[9]

Terence Fretheim

Silence for Meditation

Psalm Fragment

[God] turned their rivers to blood,
so that they could not drink of their streams.
Psalm 78:44

Questions to Ponder
· What are some ways you deal with violence in the Bible?
· What are some ways that we, like Pharaoh, set ourselves up as divine?
· How is your life and faith marked by water and blood? How does your faith mark your living?

Prayer for Today

God of promise, help us as we struggle with violence in your word and in your world. Grant us peace and hope in your dear Son. Amen.

Day 10—Saturday
Water Marks Victory at Sea

> Then Moses and the Israelites sang this song to the LORD:
> "I will sing to the LORD, for he has triumphed gloriously;
>   horse and rider he has thrown into the sea.
> The LORD is my strength and my might, and he has become
>   my salvation...."
> Exodus 15:1-2

No image of the Old Testament is more emblematic of God's work as savior than the Red Sea miracle. God saves the people of Israel by opening a path through the chaotic waters for them to pass and then closes the sea, drowning the pursuing Egyptians. Once more, water both kills and brings life. Once more the water is an instrument in God's powerful hand.

How does one respond to the saving activity of God? Often as a community of faith, we sing. This is precisely what Israel does. Led by Moses and Miriam, all the people sang the glorious Song of the Sea found in Exodus 15. It is perhaps the oldest song in the Bible. To respond in song is no minor thing. To sing is to interpret, to remember, to proclaim, to create community, to praise, to give thanks.

Small wonder that Luther and so many leaders of the faith wrote and continue to write hymns. Small wonder the spirituals that arose from trying circumstances for African Americans grace our broader Christian faith tradition today. Small wonder we find our common faith as we sing hymns and songs from every nation. When the people sing, we announce to the world and to ourselves that God is active and alive, creating and redeeming. Through song the story of God's victories is kept alive in memory and worship. Through song, the story becomes the living word for future generations.

The Song of the Sea is remembered and sung throughout Scripture and beyond. It is picked up in Psalm 118, the psalm spoken in Easter worship. The book of Revelation (15:3-4) points to a vision of the Song of Moses being sung in celebration of God's defeat of the beast.

Through our songs and hymns we proclaim that God is good. How can we keep from singing?

Biblical Wisdom

> Awake, awake, put on strength, O arm of the LORD!
> ... Was it not you who dried up the sea,
>   the waters of the great deep;
> who made the depths of the sea a way for the redeemed
>   to cross over?
> So the ransomed of the LORD shall return,
>   and come to Zion with singing;
> everlasting joy shall be upon their heads;
>   they shall obtain joy and gladness,
>   and sorrow and sighing shall flee away.
>   Isaiah 51:9-11

Wisdom from the Tradition

Wade in the water, wade in the water, children,
Wade in the water, God's agoin'a trouble the water.
See that band all dressed in red, looks like the band that Moses led.
God's agoin'a trouble the water.[10]
African American Spiritual

Silence for Meditation

Psalm Fragment

> The LORD is my strength and my might;
>   he has become my salvation.
>   Psalm 118:14

Questions to Ponder

- When and how has singing been important to your life of faith?
- What are some ways you might connect the Song of the Sea to both creation and Easter?
- Who or what is pursuing you?
- How have you experienced God's saving help?

Prayer for Today

Lord, give us this day a new song to sing, that we might remember you always and give you thanks. Amen.

Day 11—Monday
Water Comes from the Rock

> *The Israelites, the whole congregation, came into the wilderness of Zin. . . .*
> *Now there was no water for the congregation; so they gathered together*
> *against Moses and against Aaron. . . . Then Moses lifted up his hand and*
> *struck the rock twice with his staff; water came out abundantly, and the*
> *congregation and their livestock drank.*
> Numbers 20:1-2, 11

Most of us have never been literally lost in a desert, but each of us knows the wilderness experience of being lost, afraid, seemingly alone and deserted, threatened with exposure or death. Wandering in the desert is a powerful metaphor for an earthly reality that nearly all of us face at some point in our lives. Sometimes we meet the devil in the wilderness; sometimes we meet God.

In much of Numbers, the people wander lost and afraid. They experience death. When the prophet Miriam dies, it seems that the water supply dries up. The very name Miriam in Hebrew (*miryam*) sounds like the word for *water* (*mayim*). After listening to the people's complaints, Moses and his brother Aaron get instructions from God. And the most astonishing act follows. Moses strikes the rock, and water comes out abundantly. Water from rock—how can this be so?

As Christians we read this story with words of Paul resounding in our ears: "they drank from the spiritual rock, . . . and the rock was Christ" (1 Corinthians 10:4). Perhaps we hear the melody "Jesus is a rock in a weary land, a shelter in the time of storm." How we gather around this rock makes a difference. We can gather around our fear, lamenting our circumstances and longing to return to the past. Or we can gather as God would have us gather—around the promise of water, even from a rock. And the rock is Christ.

Biblical Wisdom

I do not want you to be unaware, brothers and sisters, that our ancestors were all under the cloud, and all passed through the sea, and all were baptized into Moses in the cloud and in the sea, and all ate the same spiritual food, and all drank the same spiritual drink. For they drank from the spiritual rock that followed them, and the rock was Christ.
    1 Corinthians 10:1-4

Wisdom from the Tradition

Nothing in the environment promises any refreshment for the soul, but when the reality of God is encountered this longed for refreshment appears. The story of Christ, says Paul, in its failure and ignominy, is like that rock. What could look more unpromising? When struck, however, it gives us refreshment. . . . Water—a different metaphysic, a different view of reality, a spirituality which is nourishing and refreshing—can be found "in Christ."[11]
    Timothy Gorringe

Silence for Meditation

Psalm Fragment

Tremble, O earth, at the presence of the Lord,
    at the presence of the God of Jacob,
who turns the rock into a pool of water,
    the flint into a spring of water.
    Psalm 114:7-8

Questions to Ponder

· Can you think of other wilderness experiences in the Bible? What often happens in the wilderness?

· In what ways have you wandered in the wilderness? Are you still wandering?

· What signs of hope or promise (water-flowing-from-rock moments) have you experienced?

Prayer for Today

Be with us, Lord, when we are lost and afraid, wandering in the wilderness, feeling deserted. Meet us there with Christ, our rock, and meet our fears with the water of life. Amen.

Day 12—Tuesday
Water Marks Crossing to the Promised Land

> *While all Israel were crossing over on dry ground, the priests who bore the ark of the covenant of the LORD stood on dry ground in the middle of the Jordan, until the entire nation finished crossing over the Jordan. . . . The LORD said to Joshua, . . . "Take twelve stones . . . out of the middle of the Jordan." . . . Joshua said, . . . "When your children ask their parents in time to come, 'What do these stones mean?' then you shall let your children know . . . the LORD your God dried up the waters of the Jordan for you until you crossed over, as the LORD your God did to the Red Sea, . . . so that all the peoples of the earth may know that the hand of the LORD is mighty, and so that you may fear the LORD your God forever."*
>
> Joshua 3:17; 4:1, 3, 5, 21-24

Throughout history, crossing rivers or other bodies of water has marked the beginning of a significant military victory. Caesar crossed the Rubicon to establish the Roman Empire. Washington crossed the Delaware to attack the British forces. Eisenhower crossed the English Channel to hasten the Allied victory in World War II. So it is that Joshua and the Israelites crossed the Jordan River on their way to claiming the promised land.

This story, like the others, certainly begins the story of military conquest. But most striking is how clearly this event, like all others in Israel's history, is portrayed as the work of God rather than the work of the people. We see this in the miraculous way the waters of the Jordan part just as they had at the Red Sea. We see this in the setting up of twelve memorial stones from the river, marking promises to the twelve tribes. We see this in the ark of the covenant, the portable throne of God, being carried by Israel's priests. God is entering the promised land with the people as their ruler. This crossing is yet another step in the work of God fulfilling divine promises made to Abraham and Sarah and their descendants.

Crossing Jordan lives on also in the Christian tradition as one of the central ways we speak of the promise of life after death. Like Israel, we entrust our living and our dying to God's hands. We talk of death as taking our final journey. As the ark was carried and the promise marked, so shall we be carried and marked in our final days. As we cross over the Jordan, we will be similarly protected. And we will rest in the same promise that milk and honey lie on the other side.

Biblical Wisdom

> *When you pass through the waters, I will be with you;*
> *and through the rivers, they shall not overwhelm you.*
> Isaiah 43:2

Wisdom from the Tradition

On Jordan's stormy bank I stand, and cast a wishful eye
to Canaan's fair and happy land, where my possessions lie.
I am bound for the promised land, I am bound for the promised land;
oh, who will come and go with me? I am bound for the promised land.[12]
    Samuel Stennett

Silence for Meditation

Psalm Fragment

> *The sea looked and fled;*
> *Jordan turned back. . . .*
> *Why is it, O sea, that you flee?*
> *O Jordan, that you turn back?*
> Psalm 114:3, 5

Questions to Ponder

- How does the story of crossing the Jordan strike you? What puzzles, concerns, or inspires you?
- Why do you think crossing the Jordan has become connected to the promise of life after death?
- How do you remember what God has done for you?

Prayer for Today

Lord of life, be with us in our battles and our river crossings, in this life and the next. This we ask in Christ's name. Amen.

Week Three
Water Marks the Prophetic Word

Day 13
Water Marks Sin and Judgment

Day 14
Water Marks Justice

Day 15
Water Marks a Prophet's Call

Day 16
Water Marks the Flesh

Day 17
Water Marks Promise for a Thirsty Land

Day 18
Water Marks Promise for a Thirsty People

Day 13—Wednesday
Water Marks Sin and Judgment

> *For my people have committed two evils: they have forsaken me, the*
> *fountain of living water, and dug out cisterns for themselves, cracked*
> *cisterns that can hold no water.... Therefore thus says the* LORD *of hosts,*
> *the God of Israel: I am feeding this people with wormwood, and giving*
> *them poisonous water to drink.*
>   Jeremiah 2:13; 9:15

One of the most challenging realities we face is that the waters of chaos can be set loose on the world through our own behavior, our own sinful ways. The prophets of ancient Israel knew this reality well. They listened to the voice of God, always with a passion for right behavior and justice, and delivered God's often discomforting message.

Oh you, my people! says God. You, whom I have loved and saved! You are so absorbed with self-preservation that you have forsaken me, the fountain of living water. When we listen to the whole of Jeremiah 2 and beyond, we hear a devastating recital of Israel's sins: they had forgotten what God had done for them in the past; they had gone after other gods; and in place of depending on God, they had depended on alliances with the nations. As Jeremiah put it, they had gone "to Egypt, to drink the waters of the Nile . . . to Assyria, to drink the waters of the Euphrates" (2:18). They also did not do justice or defend the rights of the needy (5:28). They insisted on drinking from their own cracked cisterns rather than drinking God's living water. So, God announces that they will have poisonous water to drink.

The words of Jeremiah are so powerful that we literally feel the judgment. We know full well that this word from God is not addressed only to ancient Israel, but to us as well. We also forget all that God has done for us. We pursue our own false gods and fashion our own cracked cisterns. We neglect the needy. So it helps to remember that God's judgment delivered by the prophets was always born of love, never revenge. God's judgment was always and continues to be about turning us around, changing our behavior, calling forth our repentance—which always includes actions as well as words.

God's fountain of living water is eternal, overflowing, and always there for the drinking. Why would we want to drink from any other source?

Biblical Wisdom

Then the righteous will answer him, "Lord, when was it that we saw you hungry and gave you food, or thirsty and gave you something to drink?"'
Matthew 25:37

Wisdom from the Tradition

A prophetic response seeks a moral end in all of its activities. . . . The prophet, listening to God, has a vision of what church and society should be, and uses moral persuasion to bring about reformation.[13]

Beverly Wallace

Silence for Meditation

Psalm Fragment

He turns rivers into a desert,
springs of water into thirsty ground,
a fruitful land into a salty waste,
because of the wickedness of its inhabitants.
Psalm 107:33-34

Questions to Ponder

- What do you hear and how do you react when you hear words of judgment from the prophets?
- What kinds of "cracked cisterns" do we create? Why do we insist on drinking from them?
- What do you think of the idea that God is the source of water in both the well of judgment and the springs of life?

Prayer for Today

Give us courage, O Fountain of Living Water, to hear your righteous judgments against us. May your Spirit lead us to heed your warnings and change our ways. Amen.

Day 14—Thursday
Water Marks Justice

> *But let justice roll down like waters,*
> *and righteousness like an ever-flowing stream.*
> Amos 5:24

Of all the prophetic calls to justice, two cry most loudly to us from the pages of Scripture. One is from the prophet Micah: "What does the LORD require of you but to do justice, and to love kindness, and to walk humbly with your God?" (6:8). The other is today's verse from Amos 5. Perhaps we recall or have heard recordings of the famous "I've been to the mountaintop" speech by Martin Luther King Jr., delivered on April 3, 1968, the day before he was killed. "Who is it," he asks, "that is supposed to articulate the longings and aspirations of the people more than the preacher? Somehow the preacher must be an Amos, and say, 'Let justice roll down like waters and righteousness like a mighty stream.'" Like so many preachers before and since, King galvanized his listeners with the words of Amos.

Amos's words capture our attention and our imagination in the most positive sense. Here, it seems, the prophet uses the cry for justice as a carrot rather than a stick, though in truth the word for "justice" in Hebrew is also the word for "judgment." So Amos is also inviting judgment to roll down like waters. We cannot easily escape the truth that justice for one person is always judgment for another. Mary would have us understand this in her own song, in Luke 1:52, "He has brought down the powerful from their thrones, and lifted up the lowly."

Be it carrot or stick, Amos's cry for justice and righteousness continues to stir us. God's will for society and creation is impelling here. Perhaps it is the water calling us once again. Justice and righteousness invite us to side with the river of life rather than the flood of death. Through the words of Amos, we feel the waters of justice and righteousness in, with, and under our waters of baptism. Christ indeed has become our righteousness. He has done the work. But Christ's redemptive work calls us to the watery work of justice, to care for the good of the other, and to live as God would have us live.

Biblical Wisdom

> When the poor and needy seek water,
>> and there is none,
>> and their tongue is parched with thirst,
> I the LORD will answer them. . . .
> I will open rivers on the bare heights,
>> and fountains in the midst of the valleys;
> I will make the wilderness a pool of water,
>> and the dry land springs of water.
>> Isaiah 41:17-18

Wisdom from the Tradition

Because Israel recognized one God over all people, the love, freedom, and justice of this one God apply to all people equally. This meant in particular that God showed no partiality or favoritism for the rich and powerful against the needy.[14]

Kosuke Koyama

Silence for Meditation

Psalm Fragment

> The LORD is king! Let the earth rejoice;
>> let the many coastlands be glad!
> . . . righteousness and justice are the foundation of his throne.
>> Psalm 97:1-2

Questions to Ponder

- Why do you think Amos's words ring true?
- Can you name people whose faith has been guided by the call to do justice? If so, who?

- What connections do you see between Amos's words and the teachings of Jesus?

Prayer for Today

Change us, Lord! Help us to seek justice for all and to join with others swept up by your stream of righteousness. This we ask in Christ's name. Amen.

Day 15—Friday
Water Marks a Prophet's Call

> *But the LORD hurled a great wind upon the sea. . . . Then [the sailors] said to [Jonah], "What shall we do to you, that the sea may quiet down for us?" . . . He said to them, "Pick me up and throw me into the sea, . . . for I know it is because of me that this great storm has come upon you." . . . Then they cried out to the LORD, "Please, O LORD, we pray, do not . . . make us guilty of innocent blood." . . . So they picked Jonah up and threw him into the sea; and the sea ceased from its raging. . . . But the LORD provided a large fish to swallow up Jonah.*
> Jonah 1:4, 11-17

The book of Jonah is a book of the sea. The sea is once again an instrument of both judgment and grace in God's hand, though in unexpected ways. God's prophet is not now the hero. Jonah knows very well that the LORD "made the sea and the dry land" (1:9), but he foolishly thinks he can sail the sea to escape from the LORD. As Jonah later confesses, he wanted desperately to avoid God's call to go and be an instrument of God's mercy and grace on behalf of his enemies (4:2).

Irony fills the first chapter of Jonah's story. His escape route is turned into a death trap. God's control of stormy sea leads to the conversion of the foreign sailors on the ship. Their fear of certain destruction and LORD's judgment is turned to praise and worship of Jonah's God. They come to know God's overflowing mercy and power.

On the other hand, Jonah gets a taste of the very judgment he craves for his enemies. He is cast into the raging sea. But then the LORD appoints a big fish to save him. He believes his salvation is a sign of his own righteousness, but he very soon discovers that he is saved in order that he might fulfill the very mission of grace he had tried so hard to avoid.

This watery drama raises important questions. Are we like Jonah, thinking we are good church-going Christians who know just whom the Lord should judge? Are we like the foreign sailors, who recognize God's awesome power and seek to do what is right? Are we ready to hear God's call to go and be reconciled, even to those we distrust or dislike?

Biblical Wisdom

> *For just as Jonah was three days and three nights in the belly of the sea*
> *monster, so for three days and three nights the Son of Man will be in the*
> *heart of the earth.*
> Matthew 12:40

Wisdom from the Tradition

Such a startling reversal of roles could also come to us in our lives: the one who has been entrusted with an exalted calling is swallowed up by huge waves, while nameless strangers whose understanding of the world does not go beyond their particular trade, commit their lives to the God of that famed deserter. As readers we would have difficulty avoiding the question, which of these roles are we really playing?[15]

Hans Walter Wolff

Silence for Meditation

Psalm Fragment

> *Some went down to the sea in ships; . . .*
> *they saw the deeds of the LORD,*
> *his wondrous works in the deep. . . .*
> *he made the storm be still,*
> *and the waves of the sea were hushed.*
> Psalm 107:23-24, 29

Questions to Ponder

- How are you like Jonah?
- How have you experienced God's call?
- Do you think God's mercy is for all? Why or why not?

Prayer for Today

Lord of the sea, may the storms in our lives bring us to faith, and may you send us our own great fish to correct and to save. Amen.

Day 16—Saturday
Water Marks the Flesh

> *Elisha sent a messenger to [Naaman], saying, "Go, wash in the Jordan seven times, and . . . you shall be clean." But Naaman became angry; . . . "I thought that for me he would surely come out, and stand and call on the name of the LORD his God, and would wave his hand over the spot, and cure the leprosy! Are not . . . the rivers of Damascus better than all the waters of Israel? Could I not wash in them, and be clean?"*
>
> 2 Kings 5:10-12

Water is sometimes the instrument of healing. Naaman was the commander of the Syrian army, one of Israel's enemies. He was a mighty and successful warrior. He also had leprosy. He assumed, like so many people with riches and power, that he could use his money and prestige to buy himself a cure. So he was angry rather than grateful when Elisha offered him the gift of healing for free. Besides, were not the rivers of his more powerful land better than the waters of this insignificant and defeated nation? Only after surrendering his need for honor and control was he able to be healed. Naaman's cleansing is like a baptism of sorts. The promise of healing and new life awaits our entry into the waters.

In Luke 4:27-29, Jesus used the example of Naaman's healing to point to another reality: God's gift of healing is available to all—from the greatest to the least, from the insider to the foreign commander. This teaching was the one that scandalized the folks in Jesus' hometown. They thought that the promise was only for them and not for the Romans outside their gates, so like commander

Naaman of old. In Naaman's story, water marks two frequently repeated prophetic words from Scripture: the promise is free, and the promise is not ours to hoard.

Biblical Wisdom

"There were also many lepers in Israel in the time of the prophet Elisha, and none of them was cleansed except Naaman the Syrian." When they heard this, all in the synagogue were filled with rage. They got up, drove him out of the town, and led him to the brow of the hill on which their town was built, so that they might hurl him off the cliff.
Luke 4:27-29

Wisdom from the Tradition

It was not for nothing that Naaman of old, when suffering from leprosy, was purified upon his being baptized, but [it served] as an indication to us. For as we are lepers in sin, we are made clean, by means of the sacred water and the invocation of the Lord, from our old transgressions; being spiritually regenerated as new-born babes.[16]

Irenaeus

Silence for Meditation

Psalm Fragment

As for me, I said, "O LORD, be gracious to me;
heal me, for I have sinned against you."
Psalm 41:4

Questions to Ponder

· What are some other ways that water provides gifts of healing?
· How could baptism become a mark of exclusion rather than inclusion?
· If our culture took sabbath seriously, what would change?
· How does the story of Naaman address the question of who has access to God's healing waters?

Prayer for Today

O Lord of Life, we pray for healing for the world. Heal our own hearts as well. Amen.

Day 17—Monday
Water Marks Promise for a Thirsty Land

> *For I will pour water on the thirsty land,*
> *and streams on the dry ground;*
> *I will pour my spirit upon your descendants,*
> *and my blessing on your offspring.*
> Isaiah 44:3

Water marks God's promise not only for the people but also for the land itself. So often we imagine God's promises as being only for human beings. But throughout the Bible nature is pictured as alive, active in God's story, and needful of God's care. In Job 38:25-27, God sends rain to the desert, not because of human need but because the desert itself needs rain. In these days when we are so attuned to environmental concerns, such divine abundance touches our hearts.

In Scripture the fate of nature is also intertwined with that of humanity. In Deuteronomy 30:19-20, when God makes a covenant with Israel, heaven and earth are called upon as witnesses to that covenant. When Israel acts in obedience to God's commands, the earth is blessed. When Israel forgets her part of the covenant, when injustice marks Israel's dealings with the poor and the needy and God's demands are ignored, all of nature cries out and curses replace blessings. We are shown again and again in Scripture that the world responds to the choices we make and the actions we take.

In today's passage from Isaiah, God's covenant promise is also expanded beyond our expectations. God's promise of pouring out of real water on a thirsty land is marked as parallel to God's promise of the divine Spirit being poured out on the people. Water and Spirit are both instruments of blessing. Baptismal promises echo throughout the land, and in the words of Psalm 148 the voices of nature join with human voices in praise and thanksgiving to God.

Biblical Wisdom

"Who has cut a channel for the torrents of rain, and a way for the thunderbolt, to bring rain on a land where no one lives, on the desert, which is empty of human life, to satisfy the waste and desolate land, and to make the ground put forth grass?"

Job 38:25-27

Wisdom from the Tradition

So, in the wise Diviner's hand,
Be mine the hazel's grateful part
To feel, beneath a thirsty land,
The living waters thrill and start,
The beating of the rivulet's heart!
. . . O Love! the hazel-wand may fail,
But thou canst lend the surer spell,
That, passing over Baca's vale,
Repeats the old-time miracle,
And makes the desert-land a well.[17]

John Greenleaf Whittier

Silence for Meditation

Psalm Fragment

From your lofty abode you water the mountains;
the earth is satisfied with the fruit of your work.

Psalm 104:13

Questions to Ponder

- In what ways do you see God providing for the needs of the earth? How do we participate in this care?
- The sound of rain may be one way nature sings God's praises. How else does nature praise God?
- When have you seen or experienced the outpouring of God's Spirit?

Prayer for Today

We give you thanks, O Lord, along with the rivers and fountains and all of your thirsty land that you continue to pour out your Spirit on us, on our children, and on all of your creation. Amen.

Day 18—Tuesday
Water Marks Promise for a Thirsty People

> *Ho, everyone who thirsts, come to the waters; and you that have no money, come, buy and eat! Come, buy wine and milk without money and without price. . . . For as the rain and the snow come down from heaven, and do not return there until they have watered the earth, making it bring forth and sprout, giving seed to the sower and bread to the eater, so shall my word be that goes out from my mouth; it shall not return to me empty, but it shall accomplish that which I purpose, and succeed in the thing for which I sent it.*
>
> Isaiah 55:1, 10-11

"Ho, everyone who thirsts"—that would be all of us—"come to the waters." We all know what it feels like to experience physical thirst. We sometimes thirst for things we think we want but may well not be good for us—for riches, for status, for power, for revenge. Then again, we thirst for noble things—for love and affection, for justice and peace, for understanding, meaning, and fulfillment.

To all of these thirsts and more, the prophet Isaiah issues a stunning invitation. "Come to the waters." Perhaps we are like the leper Naaman, wondering what waters these would be and how much they might cost. To this the prophet responds, "Come, buy wine and milk without money and without price." The "waters" are free for the taking. They are given for you and will accomplish precisely what God intends for them to do.

So how shall we understand what this water is? Isaiah's invitation is shouted to a people languishing in exile in Babylon and yearning to go home. They thirst for freedom and to hear a word of God's promise that is steadfast and true. In Isaiah 40-55, the prophet describes a servant, who comes to accomplish God's redemptive purpose for the people. He calls the thirsting people to listen to his words and to believe that God's word is like rain that waters the earth; it will not return empty. With ears of faith we hear in this prophetic word a promise of another redeeming servant, the Word incarnate, Christ Jesus. In him we drink freely from the wellsprings of God's thirst-quenching water.

Biblical Wisdom

> Then he said to me, "It is done! I am the Alpha and the Omega, the beginning and the end. To the thirsty I will give water as a gift from the spring of the water of life."
> Revelation 21:6

Wisdom from the Tradition

The servant has "made many righteous" by pouring himself out to death ([Isaiah] 53:11-12). Why not, then, rejoice? Why not, then come to the waters, buy our food without price, and celebrate the eternal covenant with God? (55:1-4)[18]

> William R. Long

Silence for Meditation

Psalm Fragment

> They feast on the abundance of your house,
>   and you give them drink from the river of your delights.
> For with you is the fountain of life;
>   in your light we see light.
> Psalm 36:8-9

Questions to Ponder

- Recall times when you were really thirsty. What did it feel like to drink?
- For what do you thirst? For what might your faith community thirst?
- How will you invite others to come to the waters? How is inviting part of accomplishing what God purposes?

Prayer for Today

Lord of invitation, we give you thanks that you have met us in our thirsting and led us to Christ, our wellspring of salvation. Amen.

Week Four
Water Marks Our Life of Prayer

Day 19
Water Marks Our Tearful Lament

Day 20
Water Marks Our Confession

Day 21
Water Marks Our Yearning for God

Day 22
Water Marks Our Thanksgiving and Praise

Day 23
Water Marks the Promise

Day 24
Water Marks the GIft of the Word

Day 19—Wednesday
Water Marks Our Tearful Lament

> *I am weary with my moaning;*
> *every night I flood my bed with tears;*
> *I drench my couch with my weeping.*
> Psalm 6:6

> *By the rivers of Babylon—*
> *there we sat down and there we wept*
> *when we remembered Zion.*
> Psalm 137:1

The seas of chaos are internal as well as external. Internal chaos is marked by the salt water of our tears. Like the psalmist, we also know that the chaotic waters of grief can drench and drown us, as in a flood. The chaotic flood of tears may come, for so many reasons: personal loss, anxiety, feelings of inadequacy, depression. At such times, the psalms of lament give expression to our often confused and complicated feelings. We learn to tell the truth to God rather than pretend all is well with the world. Through the psalms our tears become our prayers, and even when our sorrow is expressed in anger, the words ring true. With the help of the Spirit we are able to give our sorrow over to God.

Israel knew full well that such sorrow was not simply confined to personal grief. Nations and communities also weep. Psalm 137 is psalm of weeping, a community lament that expresses the sorrow Israel felt because of being exiled to Babylon, the capital city of the nation that had overrun their homeland and destroyed the temple in Jerusalem. Surrounded by the taunting enemy and filled with tortured memories of the recent horrors, they cry out to God with prayers of sorrow. They ask, How can we sing the Lord's song in a foreign land? And we wonder as well: How do we sing God's praise when weighed down with worry or crushing grief?

Here is found one of the stunning realities of the faith for Israel. It is only in exile that Israel comes to know the depth of God's grace, concern, and promise. The people Israel learned that God is found in absence as well as in presence, in sorrow as well as in joy. Insight and faith were born out of the loss and sorrow.

So it was as well for the first followers of Jesus. Only after they experienced the deep sorrow of losing Jesus to death; only when they were faced with the reality of the cross of Christ, did they come to know the depths of God's love. God's power and wisdom were not fully manifest in ways they expected. Avoiding the cross was not an option. Such lessons are difficult to learn. We are not to mask our tears or pretend. In the midst of our weeping we are met by God and given hope.

Biblical Wisdom

Cry aloud to the Lord!
O wall of daughter Zion!
Let tears stream down like a torrent day and night!
Give yourself no rest,
your eyes no respite!
Lamentations 2:18

Wisdom from the Tradition

The Bible gives disciples prayers for times of anguish, prayers for times of abandonment, even prayers for sorrows that stretch beyond words. There is comfort in knowing that others have been there before us; there is grace in knowing that Christ has already been to that darkest of places.[19]

Martha Stortz

Silence for Meditation

Psalm Fragment

For you have delivered my soul from death,
my eyes from tears,
my feet from stumbling.
Psalm 116:8

Questions to Ponder

- How have you experienced sorrow and crying as a form of prayer to God?
- How do you feel about expressing your deepest frustrations or fears or even anger to God?
- Can you think of times when you have experienced the grace of God in the midst of sadness or despair? What was that experience like?

Prayer for Today

Receive our tears, O Lord. Take them to your heart and cherish the truth that is found there. Then, dear Lord, dry our tears and let us rest in you. This we ask in Christ's name. Amen.

Day 20—Thursday
Water Marks Our Confession

> *Have mercy on me, O God,*
> *according to your steadfast love;*
> *according to your abundant mercy*
> *blot out my transgressions.*
> *Wash me thoroughly from my iniquity,*
> *and cleanse me from my sin.*
> Psalm 51:1-2

A basic use of water is for washing, for cleansing. Small wonder, then, that watery cleansing also marks our lives of faith. Because we sin before God, we have need of deep cleansing. Every year on Ash Wednesday we begin the season of Lent by reciting Psalm 51, the most profound psalm of repentance in all of Scripture. The title of the psalm forever links David's sin of having committed adultery with Bathsheba to these words of repentance.

The psalm prays that God show mercy on us in three significant ways. We first pray that God blot out our transgressions, that God erase the bill of indictment from the imagined heavenly ledger of our recorded sins. Then we pray to God, "wash me." Wash me with abrasive sand like a laundress standing in a river, or like our mothers used to do, scrubbing out the dirt from our hair in the kitchen sink. Wash me thoroughly, we pray to God; wash my sins away. Finally, we pray, "purify me, Lord." Make it a rich and effective ceremonial cleansing. As we pray again in verse 7, "Purge me with hyssop, and I shall be clean; wash me, and I shall be whiter than snow." I picture a group of young Tanzanian girls I once worshiped with, all dressed in white, standing before God on their confirmation. Pronounce me clean; declare my sins forgiven before the assembly.

God is the subject of all of these verbs. Psalm 51 teaches us that even our repentance is God's work. And as our prayer for cleansing continues, we ask God to move deeper still. We ask God to replace my sin, and "create in me a clean heart, O God, and put a new and right spirit within me" (51:10). Water marks God's cleansing in our lives, a washing of repentance so that our lives and our hearts might be made new by the work of the Spirit.

Biblical Wisdom

I will sprinkle clean water upon you, and you shall be clean from all your uncleannesses, and from all your idols I will cleanse you. A new heart I will give you, and a new spirit I will put within you; and I will remove from your body the heart of stone and give you a heart of flesh.
Ezekiel 36:25-26

Wisdom from the Tradition

Now, [the psalmist] prays almost until the end of the psalm in increasing measure that he be washed and cleansed more and more. For first, grace is a beginning of washing and cleansing. . . . Now with us the situation is that Adam must get out and Christ come in. . . . For this reason there is no end of washing and cleansing in this life.[20]
Martin Luther

Silence for Meditation

Psalm Fragment

If you, O LORD, should mark iniquities,
Lord, who could stand?
But there is forgiveness with you,
so that you may be revered.
I wait for the LORD, my soul waits,
and in his word I hope.
Psalm 130:3-5

Questions to Ponder

- Have you ever been really dirty? How did it feel to wash and get clean?
- In what ways have we, as individuals or as a community, experienced the forgiveness of God as a radical cleansing?
- What do you think a "clean heart" looks like? How does a heart become clean?

Prayer for Today

God of mercy, cleanse us this day. Wash away our sins that we might go into your world refreshed and ready for the work you would have us do. This we ask in Christ's name. Amen.

Day 21—Friday
Water Marks Our Yearning for God

As a deer longs for flowing streams,
so my soul longs for you, O God.
My soul thirsts for God,
for the living God.
When shall I come and behold the face of God?
Psalm 42:1-2

We live in a time when many folks are searching, especially the young. They are thirsty for something, but uncertain of what. They are longing for meaning, fulfillment, and purpose. And they are eager. What a wonderful image for searchers is found in Psalm 42—"As a deer longs for flowing streams, so my soul longs for you, O God."

As my family and I travel in the northern parts of Minnesota, we often watch the deer. They are drawn to the water. Sometimes the deer don't even watch out for their own welfare. So drawn are they to the flowing waters of the spring thaw that they dart carelessly across the dangerous roads of civilization. Their yearning is that deep.

This careless, uncontrollable, naturally engrained yearning is precisely how our souls yearn for the living God. The root meaning for the Hebrew word *nephesh*, translated here as "soul," is "throat." That is, the throat is the metaphorical place where our souls reside. Just as the deer thirsts for water, so also our throats—our very selves, our souls—thirst for God. And just as our throats breathe in air, take in life, so also our souls—our very lives—long for the God of life, the source of life, the one who gives life.

The soul of the searcher thirsts for God. Not knowing, the searcher asks: "When shall I come and behold the face of God?" Sometimes the very best theology is found not in answers but in questions. When shall I see God? The question itself resonates with faith. The question is addressed to God.

In faith, the yearning of Psalm 42 finds an answer from Jesus. In John 7:37-38, Jesus cries out to the gathering crowds, so many unsure about what they believe, "Let anyone who is thirsty come to me." And then, surprisingly, he adds that the rivers of living water flow out of the believer's heart. The one who longs for spiritual waters, the thirsting soul, will find drink.

Biblical Wisdom

> On the last day of the festival, the great day, while Jesus was standing there, he cried out, "Let anyone who is thirsty come to me, and let the one who believes in me drink. As the scripture has said, 'Out of the believer's heart shall flow rivers of living water.'"
> John 7:37-38

Wisdom from the Tradition

It was amazing. I do not at all understand the mystery of grace—only that it meets us where we are but does not leave us where it found us. It can be received gladly or grudgingly, in big gulps or in tiny tastes, like a deer at the salt. I gobbled it, licked it, held it down between my little hooves.[21]

Anne Lamott

Silence for Meditation

Psalm Fragment

O God, you are my God, I seek you,
> *my soul thirsts for you;*
my flesh faints for you,
> *as in a dry and weary land where there is no water.*
> Psalm 63:1

Questions to Ponder

- What sort of folks do you know who are searching, yearning for God?
- Do you have your own "yearning for God" stories?
- What are some of your persistent questions about God?

Prayer for Today

For you, my God, the living God, my thirsty spirit pines. Oh, when shall I behold your face, O Majesty Divine? (*Lutheran Book of Worship* 452)

Day 22—Saturday
Water Marks Our Thanksgiving and Praise

> *He reached down from on high, he took me;*
> > *he drew me out of mighty waters.*
> > Psalm 18:16

> *Happy are those whose strength is in you,*
> > *in whose heart are the highways to Zion.*

As they go through the valley of Baca
  they make it a place of springs;
  the early rain also covers it with pools.
  Psalm 84:5-6

More than anything else, psalms are about praising God and giving thanks. Water streams its way through this thanks and praise. Through the psalms we thank God individually for saving us from the mighty waters, both literally and metaphorically. We thank God for drying our tears, for giving us refreshing water to drink. And we thank God as communities for bringing us through the waters, for bringing water to the desert, and for covering the earth with springs.

C. S. Lewis, in his *Reflections on the Psalms*, struggles with the notion that God needs our praise, as though God is an egotist craving adoration. But then Lewis comes to the dramatic realization that when we truly love another, we cannot help but express our love through praise of that person's virtues and thanksgiving for his or her presence in our lives. Praising God is like that—an expression of our love and devotion.

Psalm 84 uses the imagery of water to express just such a thought. The psalm pictures those who continually sing praises to God in the house of the Lord. They are happy, blessed. Through their praising God, their hearts become like highways to the house of prayer. Their hearts are filled with the joy of homecoming, of experiencing the return from exile in Babylon. Their joy is like those pilgrims walking home through the valley of Baca (perhaps the "dry valley" or the "valley of weeping"). Their praise transforms the dry valley into a spring-fed oasis. When we give God thanks and praise, not only is God given the glory, but we ourselves and those around us are transformed.

Biblical Wisdom

Sing to the LORD a new song,
  his praise from the end of the earth!

Let the sea roar and all that fills it,
   the coastlands and their inhabitants.
      Isaiah 42:10

Wisdom from the Tradition

The Psalmists in telling everyone to praise God are doing what all men do when they speak of what they care about. . . . I think we delight to praise what we enjoy because the praise not merely expresses but completes the enjoyment; it is its appointed consummation. It is not out of compliment that lovers keep on telling one another how beautiful they are; the delight is incomplete until it is expressed.[22]

   C. S. Lewis

Silence for Meditation

Psalm Fragment

   Sing praises to the LORD, O you his faithful ones,
      and give thanks to his holy name.
   For his anger is but for a moment;
      his favor is for a lifetime.
   Weeping may linger for the night,
      but joy comes with the morning.
         Psalm 30:4-5

Questions to Ponder

- What are some of the reasons you praise and thank God?
- Why do you think we are told in various places in the Bible that God needs our thanks and praise?
- How can praise and thanks transform times of sorrow or pain?

Prayer for Today

We give you thanks, dear Lord, for all the bounties you shower upon us. To you be honor and glory! May we take joy each day in praising your name. Amen.

Day 23—Monday
Water Marks the Promise

> *The LORD is my shepherd, I shall not want.*
> *He makes me lie down in green pastures;*
> *he leads me beside still waters;*
> *he restores my soul.*
> Psalm 23:1-3a

No psalm has been more central to the faith of American Protestants in the last two hundred years than the twenty-third psalm. It has not always been so. William Holladay has recounted the significant people who contributed to the dominance of this psalm in American Christianity, including Henry Ward Beecher, a popular and influential nineteenth century Congregational preacher, and Louisa May Alcott, author of *Little Women*. Through this psalm we think about God's presence with us through our lives of faith, about our inevitable death, and about our eternal rest. Small wonder this psalm is recited at many a bedside and many a funeral.

Central to the psalm is the image of the shepherd, which evokes images for some type of a protector king from the line of David. For Christians, the psalm calls to mind Jesus, the Good Shepherd. I still remember my first class in psalms at Union Seminary in New York City, listening to my beloved professor, Samuel Terrien, talking about the time he spent living among the Bedouin peoples. Terrien spoke of how the Bedouin shepherds would care for their sheep, leading them to safe and quiet waters where the poor, not very intelligent creatures would not fall in and drown. And when the sheep were battered about, the Bedouin would bring them into their tents and anoint their heads with medicinal oil.

So it is with us. God leads us to the waters of baptism, where we are marked with the cross of Christ. These waters renew us and sustain us for our journeys. The Good Shepherd leads us to waters that mark the divine care that surrounds us all our days, even to our final dwelling place.

Biblical Wisdom

> *For the Lamb at the center of the throne will be their shepherd,*
>> *and he will guide them to springs of the water of life,*
>> *and God will wipe away every tear from their eyes.*
>> Revelation 7:17

Wisdom from the Tradition

The twenty-third psalm is the nightingale of the psalms. It is small, of a homely feather, singing shyly out of obscurity; but, O, it has filled the air of the whole world with melodious joy, greater than the heart can conceive. Blessed be the day on which that psalm was born. . . . Nor is its work done. It will go on singing to your children and my children, and to their children, through all the generations of time; nor will it fold its wings till the last pilgrim is safe, and time ended.[23]

Henry Ward Beecher

Silence for Meditation

Psalm Fragment

> *O come, let us worship and bow down,*
>> *let us kneel before the LORD, our Maker!*
> *For he is our God,*
>> *and we are the people of his pasture,*
>> *and the sheep of his hand.*
>> Psalm 95:6-7a

Questions to Ponder

- Can you recall times in your life when the twenty-third psalm has been important to you or to someone you know?
- How does the image of God or of Jesus as shepherd speak to your life of faith?
- For you, what do the "still waters" of Psalm 23 represent?

Prayer for Today

Come, Beloved Shepherd. Lead us to your refreshing waters. Be with us now and when we die. Amen.

Day 24—Tuesday
Water Marks the Gift of the Word

> *Happy are those who do not follow the advice of the wicked,*
> *... but their delight is in the law of the L*ORD*,*
> *and on his law they meditate day and night.*
> *They are like trees planted by streams of water,*
> *which yield their fruit in its season,*
> *and their leaves do not wither.*
>   Psalm 1:1-3

Psalm 1 is expansive. Not only does it invite us into the book of Psalms, it provides a view of God's word in Scripture. Come, the psalmist bids us, discover the happiness, the blessedness of diving into Torah, day and night. The Hebrew word *Torah*, here translated "law," really means the whole of God's word in the Bible. Torah includes both our story and the ways we live into the story, just as in the first five books of the Bible the story of God's people and a description of Israel's law are all mixed together.

Psalm 1 invites us "to meditate" on Torah. We usually think of meditating as being quiet and thoughtful. But *meditate* is a word that is also used to speak of the roaring of lions and the cooing of birds. Eugene Peterson pictures meditating on God's word as a dog chewing on a bone in concentration and delight. I picture a more communal activity of rabbis bending over Scripture, weaving back and forth, all talking at once.

Such activity, says the psalmist, leads to more than we can possibly imagine. When we take delight in God's teaching, when we participate in such cooing and roaring and chewing, we become like trees. Like a tree, we students of the Bible are made alive and are kept alive by being rooted by an ever-flowing stream. We are rooted in God, in God's life-giving Spirit, in God's word in Scripture, and in God's word in Christ.

And there is more! Once our roots are fed by this ever-flowing stream, we produce both leaves and fruit. Our leaves provide both shade and shelter. Our fruit is always for the other, nourishing and reaching out. What a wonder; being rooted in the waters of God's word brings us joy and also has as its end the feeding and sheltering of the world.

Biblical Wisdom

Blessed are those who trust in the LORD,
whose trust is the LORD.
They shall be like a tree planted by water,
sending out its roots by the stream.
It shall not fear when heat comes,
and its leaves shall stay green;
in the year of drought it is not anxious,
and it does not cease to bear fruit.
Jeremiah 17:7-8

Wisdom from the Tradition

The Book of Psalms begins with a beatitude. Not a prayer or a hymn, but a statement about human existence. . . . This opening beatitude also serves as an introduction to the book. . . . The psalm is there to invite us to read and use the entire book as a guide to the blessed life. . . . For this psalm, torah is a means of grace. . . . The psalmist trusts himself to torah as a discipline of entrusting life to the Lord.[24]

James Mays

Silence for Meditation

Psalm Fragment

He sends out his command to the earth;
his word runs swiftly. . . .
He sends out his word, and melts them;
he makes his wind blow, and the waters flow.
Psalm 147:15, 18

Questions to Ponder

- Does meditating on Scripture give you joy? How so?
- What are some of the fruits of your study?
- Complete the sentence "God's Word is like . . ."

Prayer for Today

O Living Word, may studying Scripture together be our joy and our delight. Water our roots so that the fruit of our study might be the healing of the nations. Amen.

Week Five
Water Marks the Life of Christ

Day 25
Jesus Is Baptized by John

Day 26
Jesus Turns Water into Wine

Day 27
Jesus Calms the Storm and Walks on Water

Day 28
Jesus Teaches from a Boat

Day 29
Jesus Weeps over Jerusalem

Day 30
Jesus Washes the Disciples' Feet

Day 25—Wednesday
Jesus Is Baptized by John

Then Jesus came from Galilee to John at the Jordan, to be baptized by him. John would have prevented him, saying, "I need to be baptized by you, and do you come to me?" But Jesus answered him, "Let it be so now; for it is proper for us in this way to fulfill all righteousness." Then he consented. And when Jesus had been baptized, just as he came up from the water, suddenly the heavens were opened to him and he saw the Spirit of God descending like a dove and alighting on him. And a voice from heaven said, "This is my Son, the Beloved, with whom I am well pleased."
Matthew 3:13-17

Pictures of Jesus being baptized by John are everywhere. For examples, see http://www.textweek.com/art/baptism_of_Jesus.htm. Pictures abound in congregations, in museums, in great cathedrals. Why, we might ask, is this baptism so important to us? Perhaps in this event we both identify and become one with Jesus, and at the same time we see him as truly God's Son.

Like Jesus, we come to the waters to be baptized. Just as Jesus kneels or stands before John, we see ourselves also standing at, or being carried to, the font. Yet we also know most surely that his baptism is not like ours. We, like John, feel unworthy of carrying Christ's sandals. We know that Jesus is no ordinary person being baptized; he is greater by far than we are.

And as Jesus emerges from the waters, this impression of difference is magnified. Suddenly the heavens open, the Spirit of God descends like a dove, and God says from heaven, "This is my Son, the Beloved, with whom I am well pleased." Indeed something even greater than the promised Messiah of Psalm 2 is here. Certainly this water mark on Jesus is different from ours. We are not God.

Yet, even in this most exalted moment, our identification with Jesus returns. When we are baptized, we too are claimed as God's children. When we are baptized, God's Spirit descends on us, and we are named "child of God." And in our baptism, through Christ, God is most certainly pleased.

Biblical Wisdom

Here is my servant, whom I uphold,
my chosen, in whom my soul delights;
I have put my spirit upon him;
he will bring forth justice to the nations.
Isaiah 42:1

Wisdom from the Tradition

Therefore wherever anybody is being baptized according to Christ's command we should be confidently convinced that God the Father, Son, and Holy Spirit is present there, and there is pure delight, pleasure, and joy in heaven over the fact that sin is forgiven, the heavens are opened forever, and that there is no more wrath but only grace unalloyed. . . . We receive this grace on account of this Son, who bears the sins of us all upon his back and of whom the Father declares, "This is my beloved Son, etc." He is exceedingly pleased because he allowed himself to be baptized and thus drowned sin in the water and then afterwards allowed himself to be killed upon the cross.[25]

Martin Luther

Silence for Meditation

Psalm Fragment

I will tell of the decree of the LORD:
He said to me, "You are my son;
today I have begotten you."
Psalm 2:7

Questions to Ponder

· Why do you think Jesus needed to be baptized?
· In what ways is our baptism connected to that of Jesus?

Prayer for Today

We thank you, Lord, for helping us to remember our baptism each and every day. May our remembrance be marked by Christ's presence with us. Amen.

Day 26—Thursday
Jesus Turns Water into Wine

> *Now standing there were six stone water jars for the Jewish rites of*
> *purification, each holding twenty or thirty gallons. Jesus said to them, "Fill*
> *the jars with water." And they filled them up to the brim. He said to them,*
> *"Now draw some out, and take it to the chief steward." So they took it. . . .*
> *The water . . . had become wine. . . . Jesus did this, the first of his signs, in*
> *Cana of Galilee, and revealed his glory; and his disciples believed in him.*
> John 2:6-9a, 11

Jesus turning water into wine at a wedding celebration in Cana is the first of
Jesus' signs recorded in the Gospel of John. For just this one time, water is
insufficient; water is trumped by wine. This feast is marked by an overturning
of the past—the cleansing waters of purification are insufficient for the radical
cleansing of God's reign. This feast is marked by abundance—the jars are numer-
ous and huge, unexpectedly so. This feast is marked by surprise—the steward
is stunned: "Everyone serves the good wine first. . . . But you have kept the good
wine until now" (2:10). This feast is marked by hospitality—the needs of the
guests are met and surpassed. This feast is marked by revelation—Christ's glory
is revealed.

Each Sunday we are invited to a feast that exceeds the miraculous wedding
feast in Cana. We experience our own foretaste of God's kingdom feast as we
gather around the festive table and share Christ's body and blood in the bread
and wine. The opening of one of Jesus' parables captures this: "The kingdom
of heaven may be compared to a king who gave a wedding banquet for his son"
(Matthew 22:2). The miracle wine, this beginning sign of a new creation unfold-
ing, is filled with a literal foretaste of the kingdom of heaven. What a sign. What
a promise.

Imagine something so common opening our eyes and our taste buds to
the in-breaking reality of God's reign. Imagine something so common opening us to the reality that the world is a place of surprise, because God is present. We are indeed invited to a wedding feast. Are we not met by overflowing
abundance?

Biblical Wisdom

The time is surely coming, says the LORD, when the one who plows
shall overtake the one who reaps,
and the treader of grapes the one who sows the seed;
the mountains shall drip sweet wine, and all the hills shall flow with it.
Amos 9:13

Wisdom from the Tradition

In the miracle in John 2:1-11, Jesus works an unprecedented act, the transformation of many gallons of water into good, rich wine. It is a miracle of abundance,
of extravagance, of transformation and new possibilities. The grace the miracle
offers and the glimpse of Jesus' glory it provides (2:11) run outside conventional
expectations and place the reader at odds with how he or she thought the world
was ordered.[26]

Gail O'Day

Silence for Meditation

Psalm Fragment

You cause . . . wine to gladden the human heart,
oil to make the face shine,
and bread to strengthen the human heart.
Psalm 104:14-15

Questions to Ponder

- Why do you suppose turning water into wine was Jesus' first sign?
- What are the marks of a really grace-filled party?
- Where have you seen signs of God's presence in the world? In your life?

Prayer for Today

God of signs and miracles, open our eyes and surprise us this day with your gen-
erosity and grace. Amen.

Day 27—Friday
Jesus Calms the Storm and Walks on Water

A windstorm arose on the sea, so great that the boat was being swamped by the waves; . . . And they went and woke [Jesus] up, saying, "Lord, save us! We are perishing!" And he said to them, "Why are you afraid, you of little faith?" Then he got up and rebuked the winds and the sea; and there was a dead calm. They were amazed, saying, "What sort of man is this, that even the winds and the sea obey him?"
  Matthew 8:24-27

And early in the morning he came walking toward them on the sea. . . . Peter got out of the boat, started walking on the water. . . . He became frightened, and beginning to sink, he cried out, "Lord, save me!" Jesus [said] . . . to him, "You of little faith, why did you doubt?" When they got into the boat, the wind ceased. And those in the boat worshiped him, saying, "Truly you are the Son of God."
  Matthew 14:25, 29-33

Jesus was well acquainted with rough water. Matthew's Gospel reports two astonishing events that happened on the Sea of Galilee. Storms could blow up without much warning on the lake, so it's no surprise that Jesus and his disciples found themselves sailing in the midst of sudden storms. In both events, Jesus quiets the storm and calms the raging waves. Jesus acts as only God could. In his taming of the sea, Jesus reminds us of God conquering the chaotic waters of creation and opening a path for God's people to cross the Red Sea.

The disciples' response in these stormy moments is instructive. They first respond as we might expect—with fear and perhaps a bit of annoyance: How can you sleep when the storm is raging? "Lord, save us! We are perishing!" In one situation, Peter displays unexpected courage. He responds by jumping out of the boat to walk out on the water to meet Jesus, who is already strolling on the waves to their rescue. But then, like the disciples in the boat, he is overcome by fear. His fear begins to sink him like a rock.

To the fearful disciples Jesus twice responds by calling them out, You of little faith, why do you fear, why do you doubt? In spite the doubt and fear, Jesus calms the raging winds and waves. The disciples respond with amazement and perhaps a bit of faith. Their question leans in the direction of faith: What sort of man is this? Their proclamation ("Truly you are the Son of God") makes it clear they recognize the power of God in their midst.

We modern disciples experience our own storms. And we know well the reactions of annoyance, fear, and lack of faith. Can we hear the voice of Jesus calling to us in the midst of our chaotic seas: Why do you fear, why do you doubt? Can we also hear his words of assurance: See, I control the wind and the waves!

Storms will come. Some will blow up suddenly, and others will rumble ominously on the horizon before blowing through. Life's storms will produce fear and perhaps a range of other emotions. But, because we follow the one who can calm both wind and wave, fear does not have to be the last word. We are held in the hands of the very Son of God.

Biblical Wisdom

Many waters cannot quench love,
neither can floods drown it.
Song of Solomon 8:7

Wisdom from the Tradition

On rare occasions I have known the complete surrender that comes at high tide when the struggle over what—or if—I believe gives way to trust. Then, through no effort of my own, like a swimmer who knows the water will hold her, I rest in God's embrace.[27]

Susan Briehl

Silence for Meditation

Psalm Fragment

O LORD God of hosts,
who is as mighty as you, O LORD?
Your faithfulness surrounds you.

You rule the raging of the sea;
when its waves rise, you still them.
Psalm 89: 8-9

Questions to Ponder
- When you have been called upon to exhibit radical dependence on God?
- Do you think of Jesus as sharing the divine task of creation as well as redemption (saving)?
- What storm would you like to calm?

Prayer for Today
Lord, send us Jesus to calm the seas that rage all around us, and give us faith to meet all our fears. Amen.

Day 28—Saturday
Jesus Teaches from a Boat

Again he began to teach beside the sea. Such a very large crowd gathered around him that he got into a boat on the sea and sat there, while the whole crowd was beside the sea on the land.
Mark 4:1

Among the many roles Jesus plays, he is our teacher. In the Gospels, Jesus is addressed as teacher or rabbi more than any other title. One could say that Jesus is not merely *a* teacher; he is *the* teacher. He embodies the figure of divine wisdom described in the book of Proverbs, as well as in the books of Sirach and Wisdom of Solomon that appear in what is called the Apocrypha.

The Scriptures remind us that we are well served by listening carefully to *how* Jesus teaches. In Mark 1:27, as in Matthew 7:29, Jesus is said to teach as one who has authority, not like the religious leaders of the day. But Jesus does not usually teach by "lecturing." Rather, Jesus prefers to teach by telling stories, or parables. In these parables, the poor, the outcast, and the unclean become the bearers of truth. In Jesus' day and time, that means the parables subverted traditional wisdom and traditional authority.

Where Jesus teaches can be as significant as how he teaches. In Mark 4 Jesus teaches from a boat on the sea. As he stands there teaching with authority, we are reminded of the authority he displayed in stilling the storm and walking on water. His teaching from the midst of the sea takes on cosmic dimensions. Because of who he is, people, nature—the whole universe, in fact—hangs on his words. Through such teaching Jesus shows himself to have unparalleled authority.

Another dimension of this place is equally significant. When you sit on a boat in the midst of the Sea of Galilee, as I have been privileged to do, and look to the west, you see what in Jesus' day were the cities of the Jewish population. When you look to the east you see the centers of ancient Gentile populations. Jesus goes back and forth between the two, crossing boundaries, performing wonders. As he teaches from the midst of the sea he symbolically expands his mission to Gentiles as well as to Jews. The place of his teaching, as surely as his method, shows us both his wisdom and his power. We are invited to join the crowd beside the sea and listen.

Biblical Wisdom

> Jesus told the crowds all these things in parables; without a parable he told them nothing. This was to fulfill what had been spoken through the prophet:
>> "I will open my mouth to speak in parables;
>> I will proclaim what has been hidden from the foundation of the world."
> Matthew 13:34-35

Wisdom from the Tradition

Elsewhere Jesus suggests, in hyperbole, that the destructive power of the sea may be used by those who have faith (Mark 11:23) and against those who hinder faith (Mark 9:42). This destructive, chaotic power of the sea is the very power Jesus confronts and overcomes in ordering the sea by stilling the storm and walking on the water. The power Jesus manifests on the sea is akin to the power he manifests by the sea, the power of teaching and healing.[28]

Elizabeth Struthers Malbon

Silence for Meditation

Psalm Fragment

> *I will open my mouth in a parable;*
> *I will utter dark sayings from of old. . . .*
> Psalm 78:2

Questions to Ponder

- Do you have a favorite parable told by Jesus? If so, why is it meaningful to you?
- What makes Jesus' authority cosmic in scope for some and meaningless for others?
- Who was your favorite teacher, and why?

Prayer for Today

O Christ, true wisdom of God, be with us. Open our hearts, expand our minds, teach us your ways that we might respond to the power and the mercy of your profound and everlasting word. Amen.

Day 29—Monday
Jesus Weeps over Jerusalem

> *As he came near and saw the city, he wept over it, saying, "If you, even you, had only recognized on this day the things that make for peace! But now they are hidden from your eyes."*
> Luke 19:41-42

For me one of the most moving sights in all of the Holy Land is found on the Mount of Olives. There I recall joining with other visiting pilgrims to take in the view of Jerusalem from the simple chapel, Dominus Flevit, which in Latin means "The Lord Wept." A mosaic of a hen and her chickens decorates the bottom of the altar in this chapel, recalling Christ's words, "Jerusalem, Jerusalem, the city that kills the prophets and stones those who are sent to it! How often I have desired to gather your children together as a hen gathers her brood under her wings, and you were not willing!" (Luke 13:34). At this site, our tears joined with the tears of Jesus, weeping over so many things.

I thought about Jesus' tears. Jesus wept over our human incapacity for insight and change. He wept over our inability to do justice, to hear the truth that he was speaking to us, to receive those whom God sends to us, and to recognize "the things that make for peace."

It is impossible sitting there to confine the tears of Jesus to a distant past. We look out that window and see a modern city torn apart by hate and distrust, and we hear the weeping ringing in our ears. We think about our own tears. We bring our own sorrows to that place, both personal and political.

Pausing to absorb the tears of Jesus is one of the most important things we can do in our lives of faith. As we do so, we again take up the tradition of the biblical lament, telling the truth of our lives to God. But now our tears are met by divine weeping. On the one hand, Jesus weeps because of us. His weeping marks the hardness of our hearts with tears of judgment. He cries, If only! But "you were not willing."

But Jesus' tears mark us another way as well. Jesus weeps for us. His tears are tears of forgiveness falling from the cross. Jesus weeps with us. He also takes up our lamenting and makes it his own.

Biblical Wisdom

> *My eyes flow with rivers of tears*
> *because of the destruction of my people.*
> Lamentations 3:48

Wisdom from the Tradition

There's a wideness to God's mercy, like the wideness of the sea;
There's a kindness in God's justice which is more than liberty.
There is no place where earth's sorrows are more felt than up in heav'n.
There is no place where earth's failings have such kindly judgment giv'n.[29]
Frederick Faber

Silence for Meditation

Psalm Fragment

> *You have kept count of my tossings;*
> *put my tears in your bottle.*
> *Are they not in your record?*
> Psalm 56:8

Questions to Ponder

- For what or for whom did Jesus weep?
- For what or for whom do you weep?
- How can we connect the way we live our lives to the tears of Jesus?

Prayer for Today

Lord of compassion, weep for us, for our sins are many. Weep with us, for our sorrows are great. Weep for your people. Weep for your world. In your compassionate name we pray. Amen.

Day 30—Tuesday
Jesus Washes the Disciples' Feet

> *Then he poured water into a basin and began to wash the disciples' feet*
> *and to wipe them with the towel that was tied around him. . . . After he*
> *had washed their feet . . . he said to them, "Do you know what I have done*
> *to you? . . . So if I, your Lord and Teacher, have washed your feet, you also*
> *ought to wash one another's feet."*
> John 13:5, 12, 14

The topic of dirty feet does not often come up for discussion in polite company, neither today nor in the time of Jesus. But foot washing was a common practice done before sitting down to share a common meal in Jesus' day. Walking dirt roads in bare feet or sandals piled on layers of grime. Foot-washing was usually a personal task, which even the lowliest of servants could not be compelled to do for someone else.

So when Jesus takes it upon himself to clean the feet of his disciples, we understand Peter's shock and disgust. To Jesus he says, "You will never wash my feet" (13:8). Peter is well aware that those of higher status should not serve those of lower status. But Jesus is not interested in social norms. He kneels to wash the feet of the disciples, and in so doing the depth of his hospitality and service undermines all issues of status and transforms the host. As he will ultimately do on the cross, Jesus takes the form of a servant (see Philippians 2:5-8).

Water invites us once again to consider our calling. The water of foot-washing evens the playing field. No one is lesser or greater. Or to be more precise, to become greater we need to become less, to become servants to others. We are invited to put aside all pretentions of grandeur. And the astonishing outcome is our own transformation. We become most like Jesus, our Messiah, when we become most like a servant. We do what Jesus asks us to do—wash the feet of others. Our service becomes a watermark of participation in the life and death of Jesus.

Biblical Wisdom

> Let the same mind be in you that was in Christ Jesus,
> who, though he was in the form of God, . . .
> humbled himself
> and became obedient to the point of death—
> even death on a cross.
> Philippians 2:5, 8

Wisdom from the Tradition

As the Midrash Mekilta on Exodus 21:2 tells us, the washing of a master's feet could not be required of a Jewish slave. As a sign of devotion, however, occasionally disciples would render this service to their teacher or rabbi. . . . Thus, in the footwashing Jesus humiliates himself and takes on the form of a servant.[30]

Raymond Brown

Silence for Meditation

Psalm Fragment

He leads the humble in what is right,
and teaches the humble his way.
Psalm 25:9

Questions to Ponder

- What do we learn about Jesus when he takes up the water basin and washes the disciples' feet?
- Has anyone ever stooped to serve you? Did you deserve it? Why?
- In what ways can we serve others in the spirit of foot washing?

Prayer for Today

Lord Jesus, we are humbled that you have loved us so much that you took upon yourself the form of a servant, washed our feet, and even died for our sake. May we serve others as you have served us. Amen.

Week Six
Water Marks the Followers of Christ

Day 31—Wednesday
The Disciples Are Fishermen

When he had finished speaking, he said to Simon, "Put out into the deep water and let down your nets for a catch." . . . When they had done this, they caught so many fish that their nets were beginning to break. . . . But when Simon Peter saw it, he fell down at Jesus' knees, saying, "Go away from me, Lord, for I am a sinful man!" For he and all who were with him were amazed at the catch of fish that they had taken; and so also were James and John, sons of Zebedee, who were partners with Simon. Then Jesus said to Simon, "Do not be afraid; from now on you will be catching people."
Luke 5:4, 6, 8-10

For some folks the sea is the place where they work. The fish of streams and lakes and sea become the source of sustenance and income for those who fish the waters. In Jesus' day, fishing was the major industry of the Galilee. So it is that Jesus naturally went to the fishermen in the midst of their daily work and issued them a divine call. Jesus, it seems, calls ordinary folk in the midst of their ordinary lives. Throughout the Bible we find stories of God calling people: Abraham, Moses, Samuel, and the prophets. They all tend to be called unexpectedly out of their ordinary lives. And they tend to object to the call. Peter here reminds us of Isaiah, who responded to his call with a cry, "Woe is me! I am lost, for I am a man of unclean lips, and I live among a people of unclean lips" (Isaiah 6:5). When God calls us, we suddenly become aware of our own lack of talent and our overabundance of sin.

But God always responds with assuring words: Do not be afraid. . . . I will be with you. And what is more, God always gives us a job, a mission. The mission God gives to the disciples on that great fishing day becomes our mission as well. Jesus tells them, tells us, that our fishing days have a new objective. We are called to call others to come and see and taste and know the new reality, overflowing with an abundance of fish.

Biblical Wisdom

"Again, the kingdom of heaven is like a net that was thrown into the sea and caught fish of every kind; when it was full, they drew it ashore, sat down, and put the good into baskets but threw out the bad."
Matthew 13:47-48

Wisdom from the Tradition

You have come down to the lakeshore seeking neither the wise nor the wealthy,
But only asking for me to follow.
Señor, you have looked into my eyes; kindly smiling, you've called out my name.
On the sand I have abandoned my small boat; now with you, I will seek other seas.[31]
Cesáreo Gabaráin

Silence for Meditation

Psalm Fragment

Let your work be manifest to your servants,
and your glorious power to their children.
Let the favor of the Lord our God be upon us,
and prosper for us the work of our hands—
O prosper the work of our hands!
Psalm 90:16-17

Questions to Ponder

· How does Jesus call you in the midst of your daily life, or out of your daily life?
· In what ways have you taken up your callings?

Prayer for Today

Lord, we hear you call. We see the abundance you offer. Help us to share this abundance with all the world. This we ask in Christ's name. Amen.

Day 32—Thursday
The Woman at the Well Seeks the Water

> *A Samaritan woman came to draw water, and Jesus said to her, "Give me a drink."… Jesus said to her, "Everyone who drinks of this water will be thirsty again, but those who drink of the water that I will give them will never be thirsty. The water that I will give will become in them a spring of water gushing up to eternal life." The woman said to him, "Sir, give me this water, so that I may never be thirsty or have to keep coming here to draw water."*
> John 4:7, 13-15

We have seen a man meeting a woman at a well before (see Day 8). These encounters often lead to marriage proposals. In Genesis 29 Jacob meets his future wife, Rachel, at a well. So our defenses are up when Jesus is suddenly left alone with a woman at this very same well. To top it off, she is Samaritan. Self-respecting Jewish folks weren't supposed to socialize with Samaritans. So this meeting at a well is highly problematic.

Jesus asks her for a drink. Is this the beginning of an intimate relationship? Well, yes, but not at all what she might have expected.

Sometimes, going with the expected holds us back. Had Jesus followed conventional expectations, he would have shunned this woman. She had been married five times and was from a "mixed race" background, so his religious expectations would have led him to view her as both morally and ethnically impure. For her part, had she followed her traditional wisdom; this Jewish man who worshiped in Jerusalem could not be the bearer of salvation. Neither Jesus nor the woman was held back by conventional wisdom. Barriers are smashed when such expectations are left behind, and the possibility of a deep relationship opens up in its stead.

Jesus doesn't offer marriage to this woman from Samaria. Rather, he offers something even more lasting. He offers living, fresh, gushing water that gives abundant and everlasting life. He offers to quench a thirst that is far deeper than the thirst that had brought her to the well in the first place. And through openness to the other, curiosity about the unknown, and questioning the possible and conventional, she willingly asks for this water. Having been water-marked forever, she runs to share the good news with her people. "Come and see," she cries to them—and to us.

Biblical Wisdom

With joy you will draw water from the wells of salvation. And you will say in that day:
> *Give thanks to the LORD,*
>> *call on his name;*
> *make known his deeds*
>> *among the nations.*
Isaiah 12:3-4

Wisdom from the Tradition

The woman straightway believed, showing herself much wiser than Nicodemus. . . . For he when he heard ten thousand such things neither invited any others to this hearing, nor himself spake forth openly; but she exhibited the actions of an Apostle, preaching the Gospel to all, and calling them to Jesus, and drawing a whole city forth to Him.[32]

St. John Chrysostom

Silence for Meditation

Psalm Fragment

> *O taste and see that the LORD is good;*
>> *happy are those who take refuge in him.*
Psalm 34:8

Questions to Ponder

- When have you been surprised in your life that things are not as they seem?
- What are some other ways that this story of Jesus and the Samaritan woman speaks to you?
- How would describe what Jesus' "living water" is to someone who had never heard of it?

Prayer for Today

We give you thanks, O Living Water, that you have met us wherever we are and have quenched our thirst. May we respond with openness and with joy and invite others to do the same. Amen.

Day 33—Friday
The Man Born Blind Is Healed

> As [Jesus] walked along, he saw a man blind from birth. . . . [Jesus said,] "As long as I am in the world, I am the light of the world." When he had said this, he spat on the ground and made mud with the saliva and spread the mud on the man's eyes, saying to him, "Go, wash in the pool of Siloam" (which means Sent). Then he went and washed and came back able to see.
>
> John 9:1, 5-7

John cannot get enough of telling us water stories. From stories of the baptism of Jesus (John 1) to the wedding at Cana (John 2) to John the Baptist (John 3) to the Samaritan Woman (John 4) to the ill man beside the pool at Beth-zatha (John 5) to walking on the water (John 6) to proclaiming the rivers of living water (John 7) and now to the story of the man born blind, John reveals to us who Jesus is through stories of water.

In John 9 the man blind from birth receives a double watermark. First, Jesus makes mud, the stuff of creation, out of his own saliva. While the spit of another would be considered unclean, when it comes from Jesus it becomes something altogether different. The man is then sent to wash in the pool of Siloam, fed by the waters of the Gihon spring, that remembrance of Eden's garden (Genesis 2:13). The combined waters become the waters of life and healing, showing Jesus to be the source of both. The man born blind now sees. And we see as well.

We see the Messiah, Jesus, our healer and Lord.

All of these water stories lead us, as surely as they led the original recipients of these signs, to a deep experience of the power of personal encounter with

Christ. Time after time we are given drink, rebirth, healing, insight, refreshment, and new life. Like those who encountered Jesus in person, we are led to the waters. These water signs become for us signs of personal forgiveness and healing. These encounters invite us to view our lives and the world around us in a new light. Christ's light.

Biblical Wisdom

> *Then the eyes of the blind shall be opened,*
> *and the ears of the deaf unstopped;*
> *then the lame shall leap like a deer,*
> *and the tongue of the speechless sing for joy.*
> *For waters shall break forth in the wilderness,*
> *and streams in the desert;*
> *the burning sand shall become a pool,*
> *and the thirsty ground springs of water.*
> Isaiah 35:5-7

Wisdom from the Tradition

In the great Johannine narratives, Jesus converses with Nicodemus about birth from above, Jesus encounters the woman of Samaria at the well, and Jesus heals the man born blind, who washes away his blindness in the pool of Siloam. The lectionary's Lenten emphasis focuses not on what happened to Jesus long ago, but on what happens to Christians as they return daily to the water. The Spirit of Christ is bringing new life to the entire baptized community.[33]

Gail Ramshaw

Silence for Meditation

Psalm Fragment

> *The Lord opens the eyes of the blind.*
> *The Lord lifts up those who are bowed down.*
> Psalm 146:8

Questions to Ponder

- As you think of all the stories of John about Jesus and water, which encounter stands out the most? Why?
- How do your eyes need to be opened? What do you want to see more clearly?
- Where do you seek healing? How do you respond to those who seek healing?

Prayer for Today

Healing Lord, in remembrance of our baptism, let our lives this day serve as witnesses to the new sight you have given us. In Christ's name. Amen.

Day 34—Saturday
A Woman Washes Jesus' Feet

> *And a woman in the city, who was a sinner, having learned that he was eating in the Pharisee's house, brought an alabaster jar of ointment. She stood behind him at his feet, weeping, and began to bathe his feet with her tears and to dry them with her hair ... and anointing them with the ointment.*
> *... Then turning toward the woman, he said to Simon, "Do you see this woman? I entered your house; you gave me no water for my feet, but she has bathed my feet with her tears and dried them with her hair. ..."*
> *Then [Jesus] said to her, "Your sins are forgiven. ... Your faith has saved you; go in peace."*
> Luke 7:37-38, 44, 48, 50

This story of the woman with the alabaster jar is among the most moving of all the stories in the Gospels. Picture this woman with a questionable past entering uninvited into the house of a respectable community leader. She is so driven by her faith in and love for Jesus that she cannot be restrained. She bathes his feet with her tears, transforming the chaotic water of her personal lament into the extravagant waters of hospitality.

Her actions—from washing with tears to drying with hair to anointing with costly oil—are so lavish that she, this unnamed intruder, becomes the true host of the feast. Jesus indeed feasts with outcasts and sinners! And with her tears and her anointing, this woman foreshadows Christ's death; her hospitality becomes the rites of burial. Jesus notes her actions and marks them with divine forgiveness. Her faith leads to peace and wholeness.

I can think of no better model for us in our devotional life. We too should be undeterred by false boundaries. Confession of sins and devotion to Christ, rather than respectability, are our preludes to the banqueting table. We could do no better than to gather up our past sins and regrets and tears and look to exchange them for service of extraordinary hospitality and welcome. We might well bring our own alabaster jars filled with oil. In this season of Lent, remembering and marking the death of Christ in the midst of life is a central part of our calling.

Biblical Wisdom

> The women who had come with him from Galilee followed, and they saw the tomb and how his body was laid. Then they returned, and prepared spices and ointments.
> Luke 23:55-56

Wisdom from the Tradition

Within the narrative, the woman shows extraordinary behavior. There is no doubt that she would not have been welcomed at the dinner party. Yet, on her own initiative, she takes the risk of entering a males-only gathering, a woman deemed unclean in a Pharisaic meal because her gratitude is too great to be contained within ordinary boundaries. We do not know her future either. How like us these characters are, in having encountered Jesus, yet needing to ponder and live from such an encounter in the uncharted waters of an unknown future.[34]

Sarah Henrich

Silence for Meditation

Psalm Fragment

May those who sow in tears
reap with shouts of joy.
Those who go out weeping,
bearing the seed for sowing,
shall come home with shouts of joy,
carrying their sheaves.
Psalm 126:5-6

Questions to Ponder

· How do tears function in this woman's story?
· In what ways are we like this woman, and how are we like Simon, the host?
· Why does Jesus socialize with sinners? What does this mean for people of faith?

Prayer for Today

Christ, our Lord, may our tears be put to your service, no matter the cost. Amen.

Day 35—Monday
Philip Baptizes the Ethiopian Eunuch

The eunuch asked Philip, "About whom, may I ask you, does the prophet say this, about himself or about someone else?" Then Philip began to speak, and starting with this scripture, he proclaimed to him the good news about Jesus. As they were going along the road, they came to some water; and the eunuch said, "Look, here is water! What is to prevent me from being baptized?"
Acts 8:34-36

Consider the eunuch of Acts 8. He is an Ethiopian court official, a man of position and intrigue. He is searching the scriptures of a foreign people, the Jews. He is open to hearing the truth from a tradition not his own. He is looking for understanding and also perhaps for a relationship with God. Had he been reading Deuteronomy 23:1 he would have learned that as a eunuch he was forbidden to enter the assembly of the Lord. But he is reading from the prophet Isaiah about a lamb led silently to his death. He is not able to grasp its meaning.

At that moment the angel-directed Philip comes along, and this foreign dignitary invites him to join him as both guest and teacher. Philip opens up the scriptures to the Ethiopian. The passage from Isaiah he reads speaks of a servant who suffers on behalf of his people. The suffering servant, Philip reveals, is Jesus, the one who has died and now is risen. The good news captures the eunuch, who orders the chariot to stop at the first sign of water. He exclaims, "Look, here is water! What is to prevent me from being baptized?"

And this question is directed as much to us, the present hearers of this word, as it was to Philip on that road long ago. In reality, many things prevent people from coming to the renewing waters of baptism. But because Jesus has taken on the sins of the world, nothing need stand in their way. The Holy Spirit calls and sends new Philips to tell the Jesus story and to lead new seekers to the waters. What's to prevent it?

Biblical Wisdom

Do not let the eunuch say, "I am just a dry tree."
For thus says the LORD:
To the eunuchs who keep my sabbaths,
    who choose the things that please me
    and hold fast my covenant,
I will give, in my house and within my walls,
    a monument and a name
    better than sons and daughters;
I will give them an everlasting name that shall not be cut off.
    Isaiah 56:3-5

Wisdom from the Tradition

Luke's audience would be fascinated by this Ethiopian. . . . Here is a person from an exotic land, the edge of the world, Timbuktu, someone whose dark skin made him an object of wonder and admiration among Jews and Romans. . . . Here is an earnest inquirer who reaches out and is graciously included into the actions of God.[35]
    William Willimon

Silence for Meditation

Psalm Fragment

> Let Ethiopia hasten to stretch out its hands to God.
> Sing to God, O kingdoms of the earth;
>> sing praises to the Lord.
>> Psalm 68:31b-32

Questions to Ponder

- How would you have responded to the eunuch's request to be baptized?
- How does this story point to the promise of the resurrected Christ that "you will be my witnesses . . . to the ends of the earth" (Act 1:8)?
- What, if anything, prevents more people from hearing the good news of Jesus and being baptized?

Prayer for Today

Lord, we give you thanks this day for those put in our path who wish to embrace your Word and be baptized. Give us courage and wisdom to lead them to you. In Christ's name. Amen.

Day 36—Tuesday
Lydia and Paul Meet by the River

> On the sabbath day we went outside the gate by the river, where we supposed there was a place of prayer; and we sat down and spoke to the women who had gathered there. A certain woman named Lydia, a worshiper of God, was listening to us; she was from the city of Thyatira and a dealer in purple cloth. The Lord opened her heart to listen eagerly to what was said by Paul. When she and her household were baptized, she urged us, saying, "If you have judged me to be faithful to the Lord, come and stay at my home." And she prevailed upon us.
> Acts 16:13-15

Here stands Lydia, like so many women, down by the river with her companions. Somehow whenever one hears of a group of women at a river, we imagine them washing clothes. Paul supposes this to be a place of prayer. God is already there, before Paul even arrives.

Lydia is a complicated figure. As a woman and a foreigner, an immigrant to this commercial center of Philippi, she stands outside the center of power, outside the gates. But as a wealthy trader, a dealer in valuable purple cloth, and head of a household, she also has power and substance. Lydia is already a worshiper of God. She and the women with her are outside the gate, away from the center of things. They are down by the river. At this river, the Lord opens her heart.

The river becomes the place of gospel proclamation. Because of this, the river then becomes the place of baptism. This place outside the gate now becomes the fountain of faith and the center of new community. The outside waters are transformed by the Spirit to bring about the rebirth of Lydia and her household. Then Lydia, the newly baptized, issues an invitation to Paul to "come and stay at my home." Paul, the proclaimer, is called on to accept hospitality, rather than give it. Lydia's home becomes the place of hospitality and fellowship.

So often we think that the newly baptized are called upon to become part of our church, part of who we already are. But in this story of Lydia and Paul, the newest member sets the table. Lydia's openness to God is matched by Paul's openness to Lydia. This is the story of the beginning of the Philippian church. I wonder if our congregations are open to similar transformation by our own newest members.

Biblical Wisdom

I thank my God every time I remember you, . . . because of your sharing in the gospel from the first day until now.
Philippians 1:3, 5

Wisdom from the Tradition

> As I went down in the river to pray studying about that good old way,
> And who shall wear the starry crown,
> Good Lord, show me the way!
> O sinners, let's go down, let's go down, come on down.
> O sinners let's go down, Down in the river to pray.[36]
>> *Traditional*

Silence for Meditation

Psalm Fragment

> *How precious is your steadfast love, O God!*
>> *All people may take refuge in the shadow of your wings.*
> *They feast on the abundance of your house,*
>> *and you give them drink from the river of your delights.*
> Psalm 36:7-8

Questions to Ponder

- What strikes you most about Lydia and Paul in this story?
- In what ways are we changed when new folks join our congregations?
- Who has been like Paul for you? Who has been like Lydia for you?

Prayer for Today

Open our hearts, Lord, as you opened the heart of Lydia. Open our churches, Lord, as Lydia opened her home. We pray in the name of Christ, who invites all. Amen.

Week Seven
Water Marks the Cross
and Resurrection

Day 37—Wednesday
Jesus Thirsts

> *After this, when Jesus knew that all was now finished, he said (in order*
> *to fulfill the scripture), "I am thirsty." A jar full of sour wine was standing*
> *there. So they put a sponge full of the wine on a branch of hyssop and*
> *held it to his mouth. When Jesus had received the wine, he said, "It is*
> *finished." Then he bowed his head and gave up his spirit.*
>
> John 19:28-30

Every Good Friday we find ourselves immersed in the extended story of Jesus' passion as told by John. We hear Jesus speak words of divine wisdom to Pilate and others, words filled with foreknowledge and divine self-identification. We watch as Jesus carries his own cross, wearing a purple robe and a crown of thorns. We listen in as he forms a new family between his mother and his beloved disciple. In this telling of his final hours, we experience Jesus as truly human and truly divine.

Jesus thirsts. We know him to be human. Like us, he knows physical thirst. We know the parched lips and dry mouth. Perhaps we hear in his words not only a thirst for liquid but a thirst for life, a primal need to have life continue. Like Jesus, we do not want this earthly life to end. In John's account, Jesus' request receives a compassionate response. The very soldiers who earlier divided his clothes now offer him a drink to quench his thirst—as if they were disciples. As we approach death, we would wish for such a response.

Jesus' thirst is also a divine thirst. His thirst fulfills the scriptures and fulfills God's gracious purpose. Jesus obediently does his part in order to reveal to us his true identity. His drink mixed with hyssop recalls for us the doorposts of the Hebrew slaves in Egypt, marked with hyssop and the blood of the lamb so that the angel of death might pass them by (Exodus 12:21-23). Behold our paschal lamb. Jesus' physical thirst is for us. His death gives us life. Thanks be to God.

Biblical Wisdom

> *Then Moses . . . said to them, "Go, . . . slaughter the passover lamb. Take a bunch of hyssop, dip it in the blood that is in the basin, and touch the lintel and the two doorposts. . . . The LORD will pass over that door and will not allow the destroyer to enter your houses to strike you down."*
>
> Exodus 12:21-23

Wisdom from the Tradition

This one-word prayer (in Greek, *dipsò*) is unique in the mosaic of prayer fragments from the cross. It is the only prayer in which Jesus expresses physical agony. . . . "I thirst" is the sacred witness that there was no "spring of water gushing up to eternal life" (John 4:14) left in him. . . . Clearly, Jesus, as he prayed from the cross, did not fail to include his physical condition, his pain expressed in his thirst.[37]

Eugene Peterson

Silence for Meditation

Psalm Fragment

> *I am poured out like water,*
> *and all my bones are out of joint;*
> *my heart is like wax;*
> *it is melted within my breast;*
> *my mouth is dried up like a potsherd,*
> *and my tongue sticks to my jaws;*
> *you lay me in the dust of death.*
>
> Psalm 22:14-15

Questions to Ponder

- Recall times you have been thirsty. What was it like?
- What do you hear when Jesus cries "I thirst" from the cross?
- For what do you thirst?

Prayer for Today

Keep us mindful this day, Lord, of all you have done for us. May we weep for your thirsting. May we remember all those who thirst around us. May we daily thirst for your living water. Amen.

Day 38—Maundy Thursday
Water Comes from Jesus' Side

> *But when they came to Jesus and saw that he was already dead, they did not break his legs. Instead, one of the soldiers pierced his side with a spear, and at once blood and water came out.*
> John 19:33-34

I cannot hear about the flow of blood and water from the side of Jesus without thinking of the crucifixion scene at the end of the movie Ben *Hur*. In it one sees water and blood flowing from the foot of the cross, presumably issuing from the side of Christ. The water mixed with blood becomes the source of healing leprosy as well as healing the hunger for war and revenge. All of the biblical images of rivers and healing waters are gathered into this single verse. The water mixed with blood becomes the river of Eden, the water flowing from the rock in the wilderness (Exodus 17:1-7), and the great river of healing water flowing from the temple foreseen by Ezekiel (Ezekiel 47:1-12). I hear the old gospel hymn "Rock of Ages, Cleft for Me" echoing around me. The new creation is begun. Jesus' body is the temple, and in his crucifixion the Spirit is unleashed into the world.

Earlier, in John 7:38-39, Jesus had promised that rivers of living water would flow from his heart and/or the heart of the believer (in the Greek one can read the verse both ways). We stand as believers at the foot of the cross. From his body flows the source of our communion drink and the water of baptismal bath. Blood and water mingled together. The promise of life and healing—for all.

Biblical Wisdom

Do you not know that all of us who have been baptized into Christ Jesus were baptized into his death? Therefore we have been buried with him by baptism into death, so that, just as Christ was raised from the dead by the glory of the Father, so we too might walk in newness of life.
Romans 6:3-4

Wisdom from the Tradition

Thus St. John pictures our dear baptism for us in this way, so that we shall not regard and look only at the clear water, for, he says, Christ comes "not with water only . . . but with the water and the blood" [1 John 5:6]. Through such words he desires to admonish us to see with spiritual eyes and see in baptism the beautiful, rosy-red blood of Christ, which flowed and poured from his holy side. And therefore he calls those who have been baptized none other than those who have been bathed and cleaned in this same rosy-red blood of Christ.[38]
Martin Luther

Silence for Meditation

Psalm Fragment

He made streams come out of the rock,
and caused waters to flow down like rivers.
Psalm 78:16

Questions to Ponder
- What images come to mind when you think of Jesus' death on the cross?
- What is the meaning of the crucifixion for your life?
- Blood and water are essential to sustain human life. What sustains your faith?

Prayer for Today

Dear God, send your Holy Spirit to help us walk in the way of the cross of Christ, who shed his lifeblood to heal and renew all. Amen.

Day 39—Good Friday
The Sea Will Be No More

> *Then I saw a new heaven and a new earth; for the first heaven and the first*
> *earth had passed away, and the sea was no more. . . .*
> *"He will wipe every tear from their eyes.*
> *Death will be no more;*
> *mourning and crying and pain will be no more,*
> *for the first things have passed away."*
> Revelation 21:1, 4

Ending a series of devotions with the book of Revelation can be tricky, because so often folks think it's about predictions of end times. But promises actually overshadow predictions in Revelation. These promises have been cascading all through the Bible, and they culminate in the glorious vision of the heavenly City of God whose center is the majestic throne of God and the Lamb. Part of the promise is this: "and the sea was no more"!

I can imagine folks who love the ocean thinking that this is a very questionable promise. But the striking absence of the sea signals for us an absence of the forces of chaos, the forces of evil, the source of monsters and sin we have seen throughout our water-marked journey through Scripture. God will not only contain the waters that threaten creation, God will banish them. God will banish as well all the monsters that have swarmed within them. And there is more! Not only are external waters of chaos banished, so also are all our internal and personal chaotic seas. Banished are tears of pain and hurt and mourning. These will be dead to us; they will pass away.

I cannot imagine such a world. But apparently God can. And we are invited to be captive to this promise. Zechariah 9:12 calls us to be "prisoners of hope." We live today, this very Good Friday, captive to the promise of God that all our chaotic seas will be no more.

Biblical Wisdom

> *He will swallow up death forever.*
>
> *Then the Lord GOD will wipe away the tears from all faces,*
> *and the disgrace of his people he will take away from all the earth,*
> *for the LORD has spoken.*
> *It will be said on that day,*
> *Lo, this is our God; we have waited for him, so that he might save us.*
>   Isaiah 25:8-9

Wisdom from the Tradition

The new creation is marked, in part, by an *absence* of powers that oppose God
and diminish life. . . . Therefore, in the new creation there is an absence of death,
mourning, crying, and pain, for all those marks of the former, fallen world have
passed away, together with the sea from which the beast arose.[39]

   Craig Koester

Silence for Meditation

Psalm Fragment

> *The LORD is king, he is robed in majesty;*
> *the LORD is robed, he is girded with strength. . . .*
> *The floods have lifted up, O LORD,*
> *the floods have lifted up their voice;*
> *the floods lift up their roaring.*
> *More majestic than the thunders of mighty waters,*
> *more majestic than the waves of the sea,*
> *majestic on high is the LORD!*
>   Psalm 93:1, 3-4

Questions to Ponder

- What would a world without the chaotic forces of evil look like?
- How might you live differently today knowing that this is God's promise to us?
- What promises give you hope and keep you going?

Prayer for Today

God of promise, as we weep today at the foot of your cross, help us live in the hope that the day will come when we will have no more cause for weeping. This we ask in the name of Christ, our Savior. Amen.

Day 40—Holy Saturday
The River from the Lamb Brings Life

> *Then the angel showed me the river of the water of life, bright as crystal, flowing from the throne of God and of the Lamb through the middle of the street of the city. On either side of the river is the tree of life with its twelve kinds of fruit, producing its fruit each month; and the leaves of the tree are for the healing of the nations. . . . The Spirit and the bride say, "Come." And let everyone who hears say, "Come." And let everyone who is thirsty come. Let anyone who wishes take the water of life as a gift.*
> Revelation 22:1-2, 17

In Revelation's final vision, the sea may be no more, but the waters have not dried up. All water is now life-giving water. Come, everyone who is thirsty. That would be all of us. Come! This gift is for you, for us. This river waters the tree of life, whose leaves are for the healing of the nations. These waters are for all people.

This vision of Revelation is perhaps my favorite water-marked vision in all of Scripture. All the promised rivers, from the streams of Eden to the Jordan to Jerusalem's Gihon Spring, all the prophetic visions from Isaiah to Ezekiel, stream together to form this one mighty stream from God to the world. For me, the vision always is accompanied by music: "Shall we gather by the river, where bright angel feet have trod, with its crystal tide forever flowing by the throne of God?" The answer is yes. We will gather together with all the saints, past and present.

I think of us gathering by this promised river every time we gather round the font to welcome a newly baptized person into our midst. I sometimes envision the waters of the river flowing through the pews and out into the streets. And the whole congregation runs out, wading in the waters and shouting, "Come, . . . anyone who wishes, take the water of life as a gift!"

Come. Join us. We are water marked!

Biblical Wisdom

Then he brought me back to the entrance of the temple; there, water was
flowing from below the threshold of the temple. . . . "On the banks, on both
sides of the river, there will grow all kinds of trees for food. Their leaves
will not wither nor their fruit fail, but they will bear fresh fruit every month,
because the water for them flows from the sanctuary. Their fruit will be
for food, and their leaves for healing."
    Ezekiel 47:1a, 12

Wisdom from the Tradition

Revelation invites these beleaguered Christians to enter into God's beloved city
as full citizens and royal heirs. After all their long days of backbreaking labor,
after hearing judgment and intimidation all around them, this culminating
vision of Revelation now gathers them together beside God's riverside, to drink
of its water of life, to find shelter beside God's majestic tree of life with its healing leaves. Revelation invites them to dream about their world in light of God's
story and God's vision for the future.[40]

  Barbara Rossing

Silence for Meditation

Psalm Fragment

He opened the rock, and water gushed out;
  it flowed through the desert like a river.
For he remembered his holy promise,
  and Abraham, his servant.
So he brought his people out with joy,
  his chosen ones with singing.
    Psalm 105:41-43

Questions to Ponder

- How might we, as a church, live into this vision and this promise?
- Do you hear the promise of Revelation 22 more as past, present, or future?
- How are you water marked?

Prayer for Today

God of Grace, we give you thanks for your healing waters. And mostly we give you thanks for your dear Son, source of the river of life. Amen.

Notes

Introduction

1   *Luther's Works* [American edition], ed. Jaroslav Pelikan, Helmut T. Lehman, and Hilton C. Oswald, 55 vols., (Philadelphia: Fortress Press; St. Louis: Concordia, 1955–1986), "A Simple Way to Pray" (1535), 43:198.

2   *Table Talk*, LW 54:378.

How to Use This Book

1   "A Brief Introduction on What to Look for and Expect in the Gospels" (1521), *LW* 31:121.

The Daily Devotions

1   *Lectures on Genesis* (1535), *LW* 1:9.

2   In *Catechetical Letters Lecture III. On Baptism. Romans vi. 3, 4 #12.

3   *Genesis* (Atlanta: John Knox, 1982) 75, 81, 85.

4   "Light Dawns on a Weary World," stanza 1 and refrain. *Evangelical Lutheran Worship* (ELW) 726. Text © 2002 GIA Publications, Inc.

5   *Genesis* (Philadelphia: Westminster, 1961) 77.

6   "Glorious Things of You Are Spoken," ELW 647, stanza 2.

7   *The Book of Exodus* (Philadelphia: Westminster, 1974) 19.

8   *The Festal Letters*, 510.

9   *Exodus* (Louisville: John Knox, 1991) 116.

10 "Wade in the Water," ELW 459, refrain and stanza 2, African American spiritual.

11 "Three texts about Moses: Numbers 12, 16, and 20," *Expository Times* (118:4, 2007) 179.

12 "On Jordan's Stormy Bank I Stand," ELW 437, stanza 1 and refrain.

13 "Hush No More!" in *Transformative Lutheran Theologies*, ed. Mary Streufert (Minneapolis: Fortress, 2010) 192.

14 *The Peoples' Companion to the Bible* (Minneapolis: Fortress Press, 2010) 69.

15 "Jonah: The Reluctant Messenger in a Threatened World," *Currents in Theology and Mission* (3:1, 1976, 8–19) 1.

16 *Fragments from the Lost Writings of Irenaeus*, 574.

17 "Hazel Blossom," stanzas 7 and 9, 1874.

18 "Slaking the Burning Thirst," www.drbilllong.com/Lectionary/Is551.

19 *A World According to God* (San Francisco: John Wiley, 2004) 78.

20 *Selected Psalms III* (1517; rev. 1525) LW 14:167.

21 *Traveling Mercies* (New York: Anchor Books, 1999) 143.

22 *Reflections on the Psalms* (San Diego: Harcourt Brace Javanovich, 1958) 95, 97.

23 *Life Thoughts* (Boston: Phillips Sampson, 1858) 8–10. Quoted in William Holladay, "How the 23rd Psalm Became an American Secular Icon" in *The Psalms through Three Thousand Years* (Minneapolis: Fortress, 1993), 359–371.

24 *Psalms* (Louisville: John Knox, 1994) 40, 42.

25 *Sermon on Matthew 3:13-17* (1540), LW 51:319.

26 *John, New Interpreter's Bible*, vol. 9 (Nashville: Abingdon, 1995) 540.

27 "Living in the Presence of God," in *On Our Way*, ed. Dorothy Bass and Susan Briehl, (Nashville: Upper Room Books, 2010) 212.

28 "The Jesus of Mark and the Sea of Galilee," *Journal of Biblical Literature* (103:3, 1984), 374.

29   "There's a Wideness in God's Mercy," ELW 587, stanza 1.

30   *The Gospel According to John, XIII–XXI*, Anchor Bible Commentary (Garden City: Doubleday, 1970) 564.

31   "You Have Come Down to the Lakeshore," ELW 817, stanza 1.

32   *Homily XXXII. John 4:13, 14*, p. 111.

33   *Treasures Old and New: Images in the Lectionary* (Minneapolis: Augsburg Fortress, 2002) 407.

34   Commentary on Luke 7:36—8:3, www.workingpreacher.org/preaching .aspx?lect_date=6/13/2010.

35   *Acts* (Louisville: John Knox, 1988) 71–72.

36   The lyrics to "Down to the River to Pray" are traditional. A recent arrangement by Alison Krauss was made popular as part of the soundtrack to the movie *O Brother, Where Art Thou?*

37   *Tell It Slant* (Grand Rapids: Eerdmans, 2008) 256–257.

38   "Sermon on Matt. 3:13-17 at the Baptism of Bernhard von Anhalt (1540)," *LW* 51:325–326.

39   *Revelation and the End of All Things* (Grand Rapids: Eerdmans, 2001) 192.

40   *The Rapture Exposed* (Boulder: Westview Press, 2004) 145–146. Also "Shall We Gather," ELW 423, stanza 1.

Bible Passages Used

Psalm 22:14-15	Day 37
Psalm 23:1-3a	Day 23
Psalm 24:1-2	Day 5
Psalm 25:9	Day 30
Psalm 29:10	Day 3
Psalm 30:4-5	Day 22
Psalm 33:6-7	Day 1
Psalm 34:8	Day 32
Psalm 36:7-8	Day 36
Psalm 36:8-9	Day 18
Psalm 41:4	Day 16
Psalm 42:1-2	Day 21
Psalm 46:1-5a	Day 6
Psalm 51:1-2	Day 20
Psalm 56:8	Day 29
Psalm 63:1	Day 21
Psalm 68:31b-32	Day 35
Psalm 74:13	Day 2
Psalm 77:19	Day 7
Psalm 78:2	Day 28
Psalm 78:16	Day 38
Psalm 78:44	Day 9
Psalm 84:5-6	Day 22
Psalm 89:8-9	Day 27
Psalm 90:16-17	Day 31
Psalm 93:1a, 3-4	Day 39
Psalm 95:6-7a	Day 23
Psalm 97:1-2	Day 14
Psalm 104:13	Day 17
Psalm 104:14-15	Day 26
Psalm 105:41-43	Day 40
Psalm 107:23-24, 29	Day 15
Psalm 107:33-34	Day 13
Psalm 107:35	Day 4